THE UPPER ROOM

Jesus' Parting Promises for Troubled Hearts

The UPPER ROOM

JOHN MACARTHUR

KRESS
BIBLICAL
RESOURCES

Kress Biblical Resources
www.kressbiblical.com

The Upper Room: Jesus' Parting Promises for Troubled Hearts

Copyright © 2014 by John F. MacArthur, Jr.

ISBN 978-1-934952-20-7

All Scripture quotations in this book, except those noted otherwise, are from The Holy Bible, English Standard Version® (ESV®), copyright © 2001 by Crossway, a publishing ministry of Good News Publishers. Used by permission. All rights reserved.

Quotations marked KJV are from the King James Version of the Bible.

Cover design by Kirk DouPonce, DogEared Design
Interior design and typeset by Katherine Lloyd, The DESK

Printed in the United States of America

Contents

Acknowledgments

———⋙⋘———

For more than three decades Phil Johnson has pulled together material from transcripts of my sermons to be edited and recast in book form. The first edition of this book was only the second project we ever worked on together, and I'm thankful for Phil's work on this new edition as well. I'm also grateful for the Lord's grace in giving us such an enduring partnership.

Profound thanks also to Rick Kress for having the vision and persistence to see this new edition become a reality. He has patiently endured more than the usual number of last-minute title changes and other shifts and turns in the road. But I'm more than pleased with the result and indebted to Rick for all he has done to bring this important study back into print.

Introduction

———✦———

Without question, some of the most poignant, powerful teaching in Jesus' entire earthly ministry took place on the last evening He spent alone with His disciples. The occasion was the Passover meal, commonly known as the Last Supper. Jesus' public ministry to the masses was now over. He was about to be arrested and put on trial, and He knew it. On the following day, He would give His life as a payment for others' sin. And thus on this final evening before being nailed to the cross, He turned His attention to the apostles alone.

This climactic, highly focused session of intensely personal discipleship and teaching covers four chapters in John's gospel, but it all occurred in a brief period spanning (at most) a few hours. The scene was a private setting—an "upper room." This was a borrowed or rented banqueting room atop some shop or large family dwelling in Jerusalem. Many such venues in and around the city were kept specifically for the use of pilgrims and out-of-towners who came in large waves several times a year to celebrate the various religious feasts.

John 13–16 is the most complete record of what occurred and what was said that evening. Jesus was essentially giving His disciples—and consequently all believers throughout history—His last will and testament. The promises and privileges Jesus outlines in these chapters constitute a rich storehouse of spiritual blessings, given to every believer in Christ. This is Christ's legacy, bequeathed to the church.

His words are intimate, personal, and full of profound love for those He calls His own. The atmosphere that evening was full of pathos.

As you read through this study, I encourage you to keep that context in mind. This book is not intended as an academic analysis. It is not a matter-of-fact chronicle of events set in order merely for historical purposes. This is some of the most vital and applicable truth in the New Testament. It was inspired by the Holy Spirit and recorded by the apostle John—not to satisfy someone's intellectual curiosity, but to encourage and equip Christ's true disciples for service and sanctification in the midst of a crooked and twisted generation, so that they might shine as lights in the world (cf. Philippians 2:15).

My hope in offering this book is that those who know Jesus Christ as Lord and Savior will grow in understanding the riches that are ours because of His love. For those who may not yet know Him, my prayer is that the Lord will draw you through this study of His Word and by the truth of the gospel to embrace Christ with your whole heart as Lord and Savior and friend. Regardless of who you are or what circumstances brought you here, may the Spirit of God impress on you the importance of giving your all to Him who freely gave His all for His people.

———✕———

One

THE HUMILITY
OF LOVE

We live in an egotistical, narcissistic generation. Our culture is obsessed with self-esteem, self-love, self-fulfillment, and every conceivable kind of selfish pursuit. We are routinely force-fed information about celebrities who are famous merely for being famous. And practically everyone, it seems, craves that kind of fame and recognition. People relentlessly promote themselves, praise themselves, and put themselves first. The current gauge of self-worth is the number of followers you have on your Facebook page or your Twitter feed, and no detail of life is too mundane or too trivial to be shared with the world via these ubiquitous Internet social media. Obsession with oneself is not only deemed acceptable nowadays; it is considered normal behavior. Our culture has made pride a virtue and humility a weakness.

This preoccupation with self and self-promotion is unspeakably destructive. When people are committed first of all to self, relationships disintegrate. Human society cannot survive long without healthy, lasting relationships. Indeed, right now we are watching the crumbling of the very foundations upon which society is built, as friendships, marriages, and families fall apart. Human pride is the evil root that underlies so many failed relationships. And yet our culture stubbornly and deliberately fosters pride, as if it were something noble.

Sadly, a shameless preoccupation with self has found its way into the church, too. I recall reading and reviewing a best-selling book by a famous pastor more than three decades ago, in which he argued that humanity's real problem is not sin at all, but a tragic lack of self-esteem. People don't think highly enough of themselves, he said (against a galaxy of evidence to the contrary). He was convinced that if pastors would begin to preach whole sermons encouraging self-esteem and work to build up everyone's self-image, it would reform the church, redeem the world, and spark a revolution that would rival the Protestant Reformation.

That struck me as incredibly far-fetched when I first read it, but over the years that kind of thinking has gained a frightening degree of acceptance among professing Christians. Self-esteem, self-image, self-fulfillment, self-confidence, self-help, and other expressions of selfism have become dominant themes in many supposedly evangelical communities. Of course, most of them aren't true churches at all but cults of self-centeredness, self-aggrandizement, arrogance, or worldliness. The selfism they are spreading is a whole different religion, diametrically opposed to the teaching of Christ.

Scripture is clear: pride and self-centeredness are hostile to true, Christlike godliness. Jesus repeatedly and emphatically condemned pride. Both His life and His teaching constantly exalted the virtue of humility.

Nowhere is that more clear than in John 13.

"He Loved Them to the End"

Chapter 13 marks a transition in John's gospel and a key turning point in the ministry of Jesus Christ. His public ministry to the people of

Israel had run its course and ended in their complete and final rejection of Him as Messiah. On the first day of the week, Jesus had entered Jerusalem in triumph to the enthusiastic shouts of the people. Yet they never truly understood His ministry and His message. The Passover season had arrived, and by Friday He would be utterly rejected and publicly condemned to die. God, however, would turn His execution into the great and final sacrifice for sin, and Jesus would die as the true Passover Lamb.

He had come to "His own"—His chosen nation, Israel—but "his own people did not receive him" (John 1:11). So He turned away from public ministry to the intimate fellowship of His most committed disciples.

Now it was the day before Jesus' death. In less than twenty-four hours He would bear the awful weight of guilt for a world of sins He did not even commit. He would suffer ruthlessly at the hands of cruel men and be nailed to a cross. He would further be subjected to the full measure of God's wrath against humanity's sin. *That* was the terrible cup He would be given to drink.

Fully knowing all that was coming, Jesus was nevertheless preoccupied with others' needs. We know what filled His mind and heart that evening, because it is reflected in what He spent those hours in the upper room talking about. Specifically, He immersed Himself in personal ministry to twelve men. He was consumed with the task of strengthening, reassuring, and preparing them for the trial they would soon endure—and a lifetime of ministry that would follow. And one of the twelve was a traitor.

This shows the personal, self-sacrificial, gracious nature of Jesus' love. These were literally the last hours before He would die, and Jesus knew full well "all that would happen to him" (John 18:4). But His heart was fixed on these men—His disciples—and everything He did that night demonstrated His love for them, beginning with their entry into the upper room. John records this graphic account of what happened:

> Now before the Feast of the Passover, when Jesus knew that his hour had come to depart out of this world to the Father, having loved his own who were in the world, he loved them to the end. During supper, when the devil had already put it into the heart of Judas Iscariot, Simon's son, to betray him, Jesus, knowing that the Father had given all things into his hands, and that he had come from God and was going back to God, rose from supper. He laid aside his outer garments, and taking a towel, tied it around his waist. Then he poured water into a basin and began to wash the disciples' feet and to wipe them with the towel that was wrapped around him.
>
> He came to Simon Peter, who said to him, "Lord, do you wash my feet?"
>
> Jesus answered him, "What I am doing you do not understand now, but afterward you will understand."
>
> Peter said to him, "You shall never wash my feet."
>
> Jesus answered him, "If I do not wash you, you have no share with me."
>
> Simon Peter said to him, "Lord, not my feet only but also my hands and my head!"
>
> Jesus said to him, "The one who has bathed does not need to wash, except for his feet, but is completely clean. And you are clean, but not every one of you." For he knew who was to betray him; that was why he said, "Not all of you are clean."
>
> When he had washed their feet and put on his outer garments and resumed his place, he said to them, "Do you under-

stand what I have done to you? You call me Teacher and Lord, and you are right, for so I am. If I then, your Lord and Teacher, have washed your feet, you also ought to wash one another's feet. For I have given you an example, that you also should do just as I have done to you. Truly, truly, I say to you, a servant is not greater than his master, nor is a messenger greater than the one who sent him. If you know these things, blessed are you if you do them. (John 13:1–17)

It is very likely that Jesus and the disciples had been keeping a low profile, staying at Bethany during this final week before the crucifixion. Having traveled on foot from there (or from anywhere near Jerusalem) they would have had to take mostly unpaved but heavily trafficked roads. Naturally, by the time they arrived, their feet were covered with dirt from the journey.

Everyone in that culture faced the same problem. On good days the roads were covered with a grimy layer of tenacious dust. On rainy days every pathway became a quagmire. Either way, no pedestrian's feet could remain filth-free. So at the entrance to every Jewish home was a large basin of water to wash visitors' feet. Normally, footwashing was regarded as a slave's task. The duty was always delegated to the lowest-ranking servant on site. When guests came, the servant was expected to go to the door and wash each traveler's feet—not a pleasant task.

In fact, this was probably the most abject duty ever performed in public. The disciples of rabbis were not even supposed to wash the feet of their masters. Footwashing was uniquely the task of a low-ranking slave.

When Jesus and His disciples arrived in the upper room there was no servant to wash their feet. It is not clear whether this was an oversight on the part of the person who owned the room, a failure attributable to one of the hired servants, a quirk of bad timing, or some other cause. What *is* clear is that it was a rather serious breach of protocol, yet not one of the disciples was willing to step into the servant's role and sacrifice his own personal pride or social status in order to see that the needs of the group were met. Jesus Himself therefore took up the towel and basin and knelt to serve the others.

Jesus had previously taught them, "If anyone would be first, he must be last of all and servant of all" (Mark 9:35). "He who is least among you all is the one who is great" (Luke 9:48). "Everyone who exalts himself will be humbled, and he who humbles himself will be exalted" (Luke 14:11). If they had simply given mind and heart to His teaching, one of the twelve would have washed the others' feet. Or they might have mutually shared the task. It could have been a beautiful expression of brotherhood and kindness. Besides, it would have been no indignity at all, but an inestimable privilege, for any of those men to wash the feet of their Lord. (Remember, in Luke 7:37–38, a woman had transformed the act of anointing Jesus' feet into a profound and memorable expression of worship.) The basin was ready. The towel was right at hand. Everything necessary was within easy reach of all of them. But not one of the twelve stepped up to the task. The idea does not seem to have occurred to them.

A parallel passage in Luke gives us some insight into just what the disciples were thinking about that evening. They were preoccupied with the issue of personal rank within their circle of fellowship. As they reclined around the table, according to Luke, "a dispute also arose among them, as to which of them was to be regarded as the greatest" (Luke 22:24).

What an appalling scene this was! What's worse is that this was not a new topic of discussion among them. It was an extension of a long-running feud between the twelve as they vied for positions of high honor.

Matthew records that months earlier, soon after Jesus' transfiguration, "the disciples came to Jesus, saying, 'Who is the greatest in the kingdom of heaven?'" (Matthew 18:1). Jesus' reply was a clear and very thorough lesson about the importance of childlike humility.

The point seems to have been lost entirely on the disciples, though. Luke records that almost immediately, "an argument arose among them as to which of them was the greatest" (Luke 9:46). Later, on the way to Jerusalem for this feast, James and John enlisted their mother, Salome, to make a special request of Jesus: "She said to him, 'Say that these two sons of mine are to sit, one at your right hand and one at your left, in your kingdom'" (Matthew 20:21). Matthew adds, "When the ten heard it, they were indignant at the two brothers" (v. 24). No doubt any one of them would have made the same request, had they thought of it.

No wonder none of them volunteered to wash feet. With arguments constantly percolating among them about who was the greatest, no one was voluntarily going to take up the towel and perform a slave's task. Jesus' repeated admonitions about the virtue of humble service seem to have made no impact whatsoever on them—even though this had been a theme of Jesus' teaching from the very beginning. Remember, it was practically the central point of the beatitudes: "The meek . . . shall inherit the earth" (Matthew 5:5). And Jesus had driven the point home again and again with personal words of admonition for the twelve, always commending humility and rebuking pride.

When, for example, the disciples became indignant with James and John because of Salome's request, "Jesus called them to him and said, 'You know that the rulers of the Gentiles lord it over them, and their great ones exercise authority over them. It shall not be so among you. But whoever would be great among you must be your servant, and whoever would be first among you must be your slave, even as the Son of Man came not to be served but to serve, and to give his life as a ransom for many'" (Matthew 20:25–28).

Now, in the upper room, He repeated Himself once more in almost identical words. "He said to them, 'The kings of the Gentiles exercise lordship over them, and those in authority over them are called benefactors. But not so with you. Rather, let the greatest among you become as the youngest, and the leader as one who serves'" (Luke 22:25–26).

If anyone in that room had a right to be thinking about the glory that would be His in the kingdom, it was Jesus. John 13:1 expressly says He "knew that his hour had come to depart out of this world to the Father." He was on a divine timetable, conscious of the fact that He soon would be glorified: "Jesus, knowing that the Father had given all things into his hands, and that he had come from God and was going back to God . . ." (v. 3).

That's when Jesus "rose from supper. He laid aside his outer garments, and taking a towel, tied it around his waist. Then he poured water into a basin and began to wash the disciples' feet and to wipe them with the towel that was wrapped around him" (John 13:4–5). Having willingly set aside the glory that was rightfully His, and in spite of the disciples' appalling selfishness, Jesus' main concern that night was to demonstrate His personal love to the twelve so that they might be secure in it.

Verse 1 says, "having loved his own who were in the world, he loved them to the end." "To the end" in the Greek text is *eis telos,* meaning, literally, that He loved them to perfection. He loved them to the uttermost. He loved them with total fullness of love.

That is the innate nature of Christ's love, and He showed it repeatedly—even in His death. "Greater love has no one than this, that someone lay down his life for his friends" (John 15:13). When Jesus was arrested, He arranged that the disciples would not be taken into custody. While He was on the cross, He made sure that John would care for His mother, Mary. He reached out to a dying thief and saved him. It is amazing that in those last hours of carrying the sins of the world, in the midst of all the pain and suffering He was bearing, He was conscious of that one would-be disciple hanging next to Him. He loves utterly, absolutely, to perfection, totally, completely, without reservation. At the moment when most men would have been wholly concerned with self, He selflessly humbled Himself to meet the needs of others. Genuine love is like that.

And here is the great lesson of this whole account: Only absolute humility can generate absolute love. It is the nature of love to be selfless, sacrificial, self-giving. In 1 Corinthians 13:5, Paul made the point that authentic love is never self-seeking. In fact, to distill all the truth of 1 Corinthians 13 into one statement, we might say that the greatest virtue of love is its humility, for it is the humility of love that proves it and makes it visible.

Christ's love and His humility are inseparable. He could not have been so consumed with a passion for serving others if He had been primarily concerned with Himself.

"Love . . . in Deed and in Truth"

How could anyone reject that kind of love? People do it all the time. Judas did. "During supper, when the devil had already put it into the heart of Judas Iscariot, Simon's son, to betray him . . . " (John 13:2). Do you see the tragedy of Judas? He was constantly basking in the light yet living in darkness; experiencing the love of Christ yet hating Him at the same time.

The contrast between Jesus and Judas is striking. And perhaps that is the very reason the Holy Spirit included verse 2 in this passage. Set against the backdrop of Judas's hatred, Jesus' love shines even brighter. We can have a better sense of the magnitude of Christ's love when we understand that in the heart of Judas was the blackest kind of hatred and rejection. The very same words of love by which Jesus gradually drew the hearts of the other disciples to Himself only pushed Judas further and further away. The teaching by which Jesus encouraged and uplifted the souls of the other disciples just seemed to drive a stake into the heart of Judas. And everything Jesus said about love must have become like chafing shackles to Judas. From his secret greed and his disappointed ambition began to spring jealousy, spite, and hatred—and now he was ready to destroy Christ, if need be.

But the more people hated Jesus and desired to hurt Him, the more it seemed He manifested kindness and mercy to them. From a human standpoint, it would be easy to understand if Jesus had treated Judas with resentment or bitterness. But Jesus met even the greatest injury with vivid expressions of loving-kindness. In a little while He would be kneeling at the feet of Judas, washing them.

Jesus waited until everyone was seated and supper was served. Then, in an unforgettable act of humility that must have stunned the disciples, He "rose from supper. He laid aside his outer garments, and taking a towel, tied it around his waist. Then he poured water into a basin and began to wash the disciples' feet and to wipe them with the towel that was wrapped around him" (John 13:4–5).

I love the picture John's description paints—with such an economy of words. With calmness and majesty, in total silence, Jesus stood up, walked over, picked up the pitcher, and poured water into the basin. He then removed His outer robe, His belt, and very likely His inner tunic—leaving Him clothed like a slave. He then put a towel around His waist and knelt to wash the feet of His disciples, one by one.

Can you imagine how that must have stung the disciples' hearts? What shame, and regret, and sorrow must have shot through them! As noted, any one of them could have had the joy and honor of kneeling and washing the feet of Jesus. But they had now squandered that opportunity. For what? A foolish argument about which of them was the greatest? I'm sure they were dumbfounded and broken-hearted as the one person in their midst who was *truly* great stooped to wash their feet. What a painful and profound lesson this was for them!

We, too, can learn from this incident. Sadly, the church is full of people who are standing on their dignity or sense of self-importance when they ought to be kneeling at the feet of their brothers and sisters. The desire for prominence is incompatible with love, death to humility, and hostile to genuine ministry. One who is proud and self-centered has no capacity for love, humility, or service. Any service he may imagine he is performing for the Lord is a total waste. If his desire is for honor and celebrity, then he is actually doing what he is doing to be seen by other people, and that was precisely the sin of the Pharisees. Jesus said of them, "Truly, I say to you, they have received their reward" (Matthew 6:2, 5, 16).

When you are tempted to think of your dignity, your prestige, or your personal "rights," open your Bible to John 13 and get a good look at Jesus—clothed as a slave, kneeling, washing dirt off the feet of sinful men who are utterly indifferent to His impending death. To go from being God in glory (v. 3) to washing the feet of self-centered, inglorious disciples (vv. 4–5) is a very long step.

Think about this: The majestic, glorious God of the universe comes to earth—that's humility. Then He kneels on the ground to wash the feet of sinful men—that's *indescribable* self-abasement. For a fisherman to wash the feet of another fisherman is a relatively small sacrifice of dignity. But that Jesus Christ, in whose heart beat the pulse of eternal deity, would stoop and wash the feet of lowly men—that is an immeasurable sacrifice. And He wasn't even nearly finished yet. He was about to die for these men.

That is the nature of genuine humility, as well as the proof of genuine love. It is far more than mere words can express. The apostle John wrote. "Let us not love in word or talk but in deed and in truth" (1 John 3:18). Authentic love is the polar opposite of swagger and bravado. It is by definition humble. Sometimes it is even silent. But it is always active.

"IF I DO NOT WASH YOU,
YOU HAVE NO SHARE WITH ME"

The narrative in John 13 gives us one of the most interesting insights into Peter's personality that we see anywhere in Scripture. As Jesus lovingly moved from disciple to disciple, He finally arrived at Peter. From a merely human perspective, of course, Peter might seem to have had the most credible claim to be the greatest of the disciples. He had some of the natural attributes we often associate with leadership, and the other disciples often followed his lead. He was the most outspoken. He clearly stood out as the primary spokesman for the group—if only because he was so quick to speak. Boasting seemed to come easily to him (cf. Matthew 26:33, 35). But his normal bombast was completely deflated when Jesus knelt before him to wash his feet. He said with a mixture of remorse and incredulity, "Lord, do you wash my feet?" (v. 6), perhaps pulling back from Jesus.

"Jesus answered him, 'What I am doing you do not understand now, but afterward you will understand'" (v. 7). At this point, Peter was still thinking that the kingdom was coming in its full earthly expression, and Jesus would be the king. How could he allow the king to wash his feet? It wasn't until after the Savior's death, resurrection, and ascension that Peter understood the full significance—and the full extent—of Jesus' humiliation.

As Jesus knelt before him in the upper room, Peter simply got bolder: "You shall never wash my feet" (v. 8). To emphasize the force of Peter's words, the New Testament uses the strongest form of negation in the Greek language: *ou mē*—a compound negative. (Unlike English and mathematical formulae, where a double negative implies a positive, this Greek construction makes the negative as emphatic as possible.) Peter began this exchange in verse 6 by calling Jesus "Lord," but he did not defer to His lordship. Though Peter might have imagined he was acting humbly by declining to have Jesus wash his feet, this was by no means a praiseworthy expression of modesty.

"Jesus answered him, 'If I do not wash you, you have no share with me'" (v. 8).

"Simon Peter said to him, 'Lord, not my feet only but also my hands and my head!'" (v. 9). That was typical of Peter—he veered from one extreme ("You shall never wash my feet") to the other ("not my feet only but also my hands and my head!").

There is profound meaning in Jesus' reply to Peter: "If I do not wash you, you have no share with me." A footwashing slave simply did not fit the typical Jewish notion of who Messiah would be and how He would come. They envisioned a conquering deliverer doling out divine judgment and fiery wrath—or at the very least, a political leader who would throw off the shackles of Rome and rule the world from a glorious throne in Jerusalem. Jesus, girded with a towel and performing a servant's task in an obscure upper room, seemed just about as far as possible from Peter's messianic expectations. (Though one day later, Jesus would stoop even lower, shattering the limits of humility.) In Peter's mind, it was not fitting for Christ to take on such a lowly task. Jesus had to make him realize that this was the very purpose for which Christ came: "not to be served but to serve, and to give his life as a ransom for many" (Matthew 20:28). If Peter could not submit to having his feet washed by Jesus, he would certainly have trouble accepting what Jesus would do for him on the cross.

There is yet another, more profound, truth in Jesus' words. He has moved from the physical illustration of washing dirt off someone's feet to the spiritual truth of cleansing guilt from the soul of a sinner. Jesus frequently taught spiritual truth in expressions and imagery borrowed from the physical world. He did it when He spoke to Nicodemus, the woman at the well, and the Pharisees. Now He does it with Peter.

He is actually speaking of spiritual cleansing—the forgiveness of sins—when He tells Peter, "If I do not wash you, you have no share with me." All true cleansing in the spiritual realm comes from Christ, and the only way anyone can be undefiled and spiritually whole is "by the washing of regeneration and renewal of the Holy Spirit" (Titus 3:5). In other words, no one has any relationship with Jesus Christ unless that person has come to Christ for forgiveness and cleansing from sin. No one can even enter into the presence of the Lord unless he first submits to that cleansing.

Peter learned that truth. He preached it himself in Acts 4:12: "There is salvation in no one else, for there is no other name under heaven given among men by which we must be saved." When a person trusts Jesus Christ as Savior, he is truly clean. Until then, he is defiled by the guilt of his own sin.

"THE ONE WHO HAS BATHED . . . IS COMPLETELY CLEAN"

Thinking that the Lord was speaking of physical cleansing, Peter offered his hands and head—everything. He still did not grasp the full spiritual meaning of Jesus' words. But he nevertheless was saying in essence, "Whatever washing You offer me that gives me a share with You, I want it."

Jesus, still speaking of spiritual washing, said. "The one who has bathed does not need to wash, except for his feet, but is completely clean. And you are clean" (John 13:10). There is a difference between a bath and a footwashing. In the culture of that day, a person would take a bath in the morning to get himself completely clean. As he went through the day he might need to wash his feet frequently—especially if he were going in and out of people's homes. But he didn't have to keep taking baths. A footwashing was sufficient to remove whatever dirt he picked up while walking.

Jesus is saying this: Once your inner person has been bathed in redemption, you are clean. You need to be continually confessing your sin and trusting Christ to keep your conscience clean and your communion with God unhindered. "If we confess our sins, he is faithful and just to forgive us our sins and to cleanse us [literally, keep on cleansing us] from all unrighteousness" (1 John 1:9). That ongoing process is the spiritual equivalent of footwashing. But as far as the gift of eternal life and your righteous standing before God are concerned, you do not need to seek "the washing of regeneration" repeatedly. It is a one-time, irreversible work of the Holy Spirit. If you are a believer, *"you are clean"* (as Jesus told Peter in verse 10). Feet that get dirty can be cleansed as frequently as necessary without requiring a complete rebathing.

Jesus knew precisely who among the disciples had been truly cleansed redemptively. Furthermore, He knew what Judas's plans for the evening were: "For he knew who was to betray him; that was why he said, 'Not all of you are clean'" (John 13:11).

If Judas had any spiritual sensitivity whatsoever, that should have convicted his heart. He surely grasped what Jesus was saying. He knew full well that he himself was not spiritually clean. It must have shocked him—and should have stunned him into reflecting on his own guilt—to realize how well Jesus knew his heart. Those words ("not all of you are clean"), combined with Jesus' washing his feet, constituted a subtle, tender, final appeal from Jesus to Judas, silently giving Judas a powerful reason to reconsider what he was planning to do. What was going through the mind of Judas as Jesus knelt washing his feet? Whatever it was, it did nothing to deter his evil plans.

"YOU ALSO OUGHT TO WASH ONE ANOTHER'S FEET"

Notice what happened after Jesus finished washing the disciples' feet:

When he had washed their feet and put on his outer garments and resumed his place, he said to them, "Do you understand what I have done to you? You call me Teacher and Lord, and you are right, for so I am. If I then, your Lord and Teacher, have washed your feet, you also ought to wash one another's feet. For I have given you an example, that you also should do just as I have done to you. Truly, truly, I say to you, a servant is not greater than his master, nor is a messenger greater than the one who sent him. If you know these things, blessed are you if you do them. (John 13:12–17)

Having inserted a parenthetical lesson on the doctrine of salvation—a sort of theological interlude dealing with the washing of regeneration and the ongoing cleansing He provides for those who trust Him—Jesus returned to the main point He was teaching His disciples: that they needed to stop fighting over who was the greatest and begin to demonstrate the humility of authentic love in their dealings with one another.

He is arguing from the greater to the lesser. If the Lord of Glory was willing to gird Himself with a towel, assume the form of a servant, take the role of the lowest slave, and wash the dirty feet of sinful disciples, it was reasonable that the disciples should be willing to wash each other's feet. The visual example Jesus taught surely did more good than one more verbal admonition about humility. This was something the disciples never forgot. (Perhaps from then on they had a contest to see who got to the water first!)

Some Christians believe that Jesus was formally instituting an ordinance for the church. Some churches practice footwashing in a ritual manner similar to the way most of us observe baptism and communion. I have no major quarrel with such a practice, but I do not believe this passage is teaching that view. Jesus was not advocating a formal, ritualistic footwashing service.

Verse 15 says, "I have given you an example, that you also should do just as I have done to you." The word *"as"* is a translation of the Greek word *kathos,* which means "according as." The idea it conveys is, "Do in like manner as I have done." If He meant to establish footwashing as a formal ordinance to be practiced in the church, He would have used the Greek word *ho,* which means "that which." Then He would have been saying, "You should do precisely what I have done to you."

He is not saying, "Do the same thing I have done." Rather, He is saying, "Treat one another the way I have treated you." In other words, the example we are to follow is not the washing of feet *per se.* It is the humility exemplified in the act. Do not minimize Jesus' lesson by trying to make a ritual of ceremonial footwashing the focal point and main objective of John 13. Jesus' *humility* is the real lesson—and it is a practical humility that governs every area of life, every day of life, in every experience of life.

The result of that kind of humility is always loving service—doing the menial and humiliating tasks for the glory of Jesus Christ. That demolishes some of the most popular ideas about what true spiritual leadership looks like.

Some people seem to think that the nearer you get to God the further you must be from humanity, but that's not true. Genuine proximity to God is epitomized in the act of serving someone else.

There was never any sacrificial service to others that Jesus was unwilling to perform. Why should we be different? We are not greater than the Lord: "Truly, truly, I say to you, a servant is not greater than his master, nor is a messenger greater than the one who sent him. If you know these things, blessed are you if you do them" (vv. 16–17).

Do you want to be blessedly fulfilled and happy? Develop a servant's heart. We are His slaves, bought with His own blood—and a slave is not greater than his master. If Jesus can step down from the glory of heaven and equality with God in order to become a man— then further humble Himself to be a slave who would wash the feet of twelve undeserving sinners, we ought to be willing to suffer *any* indignity to serve Him. That is true love, and true humility.

Two

---◇◇◇---

UNMASKING
THE BETRAYER

J udas Iscariot, who betrayed the Son of God with a kiss, is perhaps
the most despised person in the annals of human history. His personality is one of the darkest ever chronicled, and the name *Judas*
itself bears a stigma reflecting the profound scorn with which his
treachery is almost universally viewed. The New Testament writers
disdain him to such a degree that in every list of the disciples, Judas
is named last, with a curt note of contempt after his name. Throughout church history, his name and his reputation have been regarded
with pure abhorrence. In medieval art and lore he was commonly
portrayed as a grotesque character with hideous features. A few of the
gnostic cults tried unsuccessfully to turn him into a hero, rewriting
the record of his life, but the biblical record stands against all later
gnostic mythology. Judas deserves neither sympathy nor honor. The
general consensus of Christendom has always rightly regarded him as
thoroughly despicable, contemptible—the personification of everything treacherous and wicked.

Judas emerges from the background of the gospel accounts to
betray Jesus for thirty pieces of silver, and then (before the crucifixion

narratives even describe Jesus' trial before Pilate) Scripture records that Judas died in utter ignominy, apparently by his own hand. His own shame over his act of betrayal drove him to utter despair.

Matthew 27:3–5 describes what happened: "When Judas, his betrayer, saw that Jesus was condemned, he changed his mind and brought back the thirty pieces of silver to the chief priests and the elders, saying, 'I have sinned by betraying innocent blood.' They said, 'What is that to us? See to it yourself.' And throwing down the pieces of silver into the temple, he departed, and he went and hanged himself."

Acts 1:18–19 gives different details about Judas's death: "Now this man acquired a field with the reward of his wickedness, and falling headlong he burst open in the middle and all his bowels gushed out. And it became known to all the inhabitants of Jerusalem, so that the field was called in their own language Akeldama, that is, Field of Blood."

It is a mistake to regard the two accounts as contradictory. The traditional site of the "Field of Blood" is a platform of land on the lower slope of Mount Zion, well down into the Hinnom Valley, bounded by steep banks and stone cliffs on the downhill side. The reddish dirt found in that plot of land was valued by potters. Where the land drops off into the bottom of the valley below, there are dangerous shards of rock. If Judas hanged himself on a tree at the edge of a cliff and the rope slipped off the tree, a branch snapped, or someone cut him down while he was in his death throes, he would certainly have fallen headlong, and his body would have been cut open on the sharp rocks below. There is no reason, therefore, to think the descriptions of Judas's demise by Matthew and Luke are irreconcilable.

Papias, bishop of Hieropolis in the second century, wrote an account claiming that Judas survived his attempt at suicide (being discovered and cut down before he choked), but his body became infested by worms. Papias says Judas grew so large and bloated that he could not pass through a gate, even one large enough for chariots to drive through. He says Judas's eyelids became so swollen that he was blind and thus prone to headlong falls. Papias's account echoes Acts 1:18 in saying that when Judas fell his body burst, but Papias adds some revolting details. He says the discharge when Judas's corpse erupted was full of pus and maggots. It caused such a lingering stench that the place where Judas died was still uninhabitable a century later. Obviously, Papias's version of the story bears the earmarks of deliberate embellishment, but it vividly illustrates the high level of scorn for Judas in the early centuries.

When I was in seminary, I wrote a dissertation on Judas, his character, and his betrayal. Since then, I have found it extremely difficult to write or teach about the man who sold Jesus for a handful of coins. Frankly, sin is never more grotesque than it is in the life of Judas. When we study this man and his motivations, we are prying very close to the activity of Satan. But there are valuable reasons for examining Judas and his sin. For one thing, to understand Jesus' love in its fullness, it helps to look at the life of Judas. Here we learn that, despite the awfulness of Judas's sin. Jesus reached out to him with true compassion and genuine kindness. Christ showed him nothing but love, but got betrayal in return.

JESUS AND JUDAS

In John 13:18–30, Jesus and Judas come head to head. We see clearly at this point the evil of Judas contrasted with the absolute purity of Jesus Christ. The diabolical deed that had been festering in the heart of Judas—the treachery he had already begun to perpetrate—was pushed to its climax, and Jesus unmasked Judas as the betrayer.

Jesus is speaking at the beginning of this powerful passage:

I am not speaking of all of you; I know whom I have chosen. But the Scripture will be fulfilled, "He who ate my bread has lifted his heel against me." I am telling you this now, before it takes place, that when it does take place you may believe that I am he. Truly, truly, I say to you, whoever receives the one I send receives me, and whoever receives me receives the one who sent me.

After saying these things, Jesus was troubled in his spirit, and testified, "Truly, truly, I say to you, one of you will betray me." The disciples looked at one another, uncertain of whom he spoke.

One of his disciples, whom Jesus loved, was reclining at table close to Jesus, so Simon Peter motioned to him to ask Jesus of whom he was speaking.

So that disciple, leaning back against Jesus, said to him, "Lord, who is it?"

Jesus answered, "It is he to whom I will give this morsel of bread when I have dipped it." So when he had dipped the morsel, he gave it to Judas, the son of Simon Iscariot. Then after he had taken the morsel, Satan entered into him. Jesus said to him, "What you are going to do, do quickly." Now no one at the table knew why he said this to him. Some thought that, because Judas had the moneybag, Jesus was telling him, "Buy what we need for the feast," or that he should give something to the poor.

So, after receiving the morsel of bread, he immediately went out. And it was night.

There we see Jesus and Judas as the epitome of opposites: the perfect One and the absolutely wretched one; the best and the worst; the King of heaven and a hopeless reprobate (Matthew 26:24); the One who was without sin and the one whose sin was darker than any other sin on record (cf. John 19:11); the loving Savior versus the hateful betrayer. This portion of the narrative purposely sets the hard-hearted vileness of Judas against the backdrop of Jesus' tenderhearted purity to demonstrate the sharp contrast.

The story of Judas is a profoundly sad drama—probably the greatest tragedy ever lived out. He is the prime example of what it means to have opportunity and then lose it. His story becomes all the more terrible because of the glorious beginnings he had. For three years, day in and day out, he had traveled with, listened to, and worked alongside Jesus Christ. He and the other eleven disciples saw the same miracles, heard the same words, performed some of the same ministries, and were esteemed in the same way. Yet Judas did not become what the others became; he became the polar opposite. While they were growing into true apostles and saints of God, he was progressively turning into a devious, calculating tool of Satan.

Initially, Judas must have shared the same hope of the kingdom that the other disciples had. He likely believed that Jesus was indeed the true Messiah. Certainly at some point he became greedy. But it is doubtful that he joined the apostles merely for what money he could get, because they never truly had anything. "They left everything and followed him" (Luke 5:11). Perhaps his motive at the outset was just to get in on the benefits of the messianic kingdom. Whatever his character at the beginning, Judas gradually became the treacherous man who betrayed Christ; a man who had no thought for anyone but himself; a man who finally wanted only to get as much money as he could and then get away.

By the end, greed, ambition, and worldliness had crept into Judas's heart. Avarice became his besetting sin. Perhaps he was disappointed because his expectations for an earthly kingdom remained unfulfilled. Maybe he was tormented by the constant, unbearable rebuke of the presence of Christ. Surely it created a great tension in his heart to be continually in proximity to someone of such sinless purity, and yet be so thoroughly degenerate. As a secret unbeliever, he lacked any true appreciation for holiness. Perhaps, too, he began to sense that the eye of the Master could discern his real nature. All those things likely had begun to eat at him.

Whatever the reasons, Judas's life ended in absolute disaster, the greatest example of lost opportunity the world has ever seen. On the night he betrayed Jesus, he was so prepared to do Satan's bidding that the Devil was able to enter him and take complete control. A few days before, in Bethany, Judas had met with the leaders of Israel and bargained for thirty pieces of silver, the paltry price of a slave. Now, in this quiet, sacred setting—in the upper room with Jesus and his eleven faithful disciples, Judas's steely, evil will was forever fixed. He was impervious to Jesus' entreaties. Before the evening was over, Judas's evil deed would come to full fruition.

So this is the scene: the odious traitor is sitting with Jesus and the other eleven disciples at their last supper together. Judas had already initiated his plot to betray Jesus, and now he was simply looking for the best opportunity to hand his Master over to the cadre of priests and Pharisees who were seeking Jesus' life.

Jesus had already subtly revealed that He knew Judas's heart when He said, "You are clean, but not every one of you" (John 13:10). John records that Jesus "knew who was to betray him; that was why he said, 'Not all of you are clean'" (v. 11). Judas had been sitting there all through Jesus' wonderful lesson on humility, illustrated so poignantly by the washing of the disciples' feet. Jesus washed all their feet, including Judas's. The wretched hypocrite just sat there, letting the blessed Lord wash his feet, hardly able to wait until he could get his hands on those thirty coins.

Even though Jesus knew what Judas was about to do, He still washed his feet. It was only one example of the marvelous love of Jesus Christ and the way He reached out to Judas. The measures He took to win Judas, even at this late hour, made His love all the more wonderful. One might think the experience of having Jesus wash his feet would have been enough to break any man's heart. But not Judas's. He was as cold and hard and pitiless as gun metal. He was determined to sell the Master to the executioners.

THE BLESSED AND THE CURSED

Having taught by example a wonderful lesson on humility, Jesus carefully explained the significance of what He had done. He concluded His discourse by saying, "If you know these things, blessed are you if you do them" (John 13:17). "Blessed," of course, is a synonym for "happy." The person who learns how to show humble love—the one who is willing to bow to the ground and serve another believer—is the one rewarded with true happiness. When we condescend in that kind of love, when we're willing to do that menial duty for the sake of others, when we don't care about having the preeminence in every situation—*when we humble ourselves*—we will then be truly joyful and content. "Blessed [happy] are the poor in spirit . . . those who mourn . . . the meek . . . [and] the merciful" (Matthew 5:3–7). "Humble yourselves before the Lord, and he will exalt you" (James 4:10). "Clothe yourselves, all of you, with humility toward one another, for 'God opposes the proud but gives grace to the humble'" (1 Peter 5:5).

But under these circumstances Jesus could hardly speak of happiness without also mentioning the looming tragedy and unhappiness. With Judas present, our Lord needed to sound a sincere warning regarding the curse that hung over the betrayer's head. Therefore, He turned His focus from the happy disciples to the wretched traitor. And the whole tone of the discourse changes. From verses 18 to 30 the dialogue centers on Judas. This is the final confrontation between Jesus and Judas. Judas's only remaining communication with Jesus will be a smug word of greeting and a hypocritical kiss. That will come later on.

It is important to understand why Jesus brought up the subject of His betrayal at this point. Unless Jesus had in some way prepared the disciples for what was about to happen, Judas's treachery could have had a serious, adverse affect on them. If Judas had suddenly and without warning betrayed Jesus, the disciples might have concluded that Jesus wasn't all He claimed to be; otherwise He would have known that Judas was like this and never would have chosen him. So Jesus said, "I know whom I have chosen. But the Scripture will be fulfilled, 'He who ate my bread has lifted his heel against me.' I am telling you this now, before it takes place, that when it does take place you may believe that I am he" (vv. 18–19).

It would be easy to pass by that statement and miss the point. Jesus wanted to be sure they did not think He was surprised by what Judas was about to do. He therefore said in effect, "I chose Judas with my eyes wide open. It was not an accident. It was not done in ignorance. It is a fulfillment of Scripture." The specific Scripture He cited was Psalm 41:9: "Even my close friend in whom I trusted, who ate my bread, has lifted his heel against me."

In short, Jesus chose Judas because Old Testament prophecy made clear that a close friend would betray Christ. Judas's betrayal was necessary to bring about His death, which was necessary to bring about the redemption of His people. God was sovereignly fulfilling His eternal plan for redemption.

That doesn't mean God somehow forced or coerced Judas to do

something that was contrary to his desire or his nature. Judas was more than willing. God used the wrath of Judas to praise Him. Through Judas's evil deed Christ accomplished the holy sacrifice that brought salvation. Judas meant it for evil, but God used it for good (cf. Genesis 50:20).

GOD'S PLAN AND JUDAS'S PLOT

That is the consistent teaching of Scripture. The cross was by no means an impediment to God's perfect will or an interruption of His eternal purposes. On the contrary, Judas's betrayal fit right into God's sovereign, eternal, master plan for redemption. The crucifixion of Christ was precisely what the hand and the plan of God "had predestined to take place" (Acts 4:28). Jesus was "delivered up according to the definite plan and foreknowledge of God" (Acts 2:23).

But that does not alter the fact that what Judas did was supremely evil. The people screaming for Jesus' blood were acting wickedly. Indeed, the crucifixion of Christ represents the pure distillation of every possible expression of human villainy. Acts 2:23 goes on to say that Jesus was "crucified and killed by the hands of lawless men." Clearly, the fact that God used their deed for good does not erase their guilt or mitigate the sinfulness of what they did. God's sovereignty never nullifies human responsibility.

Nevertheless, when He quoted Psalm 41:9, Jesus was stressing the fact of God's sovereignty, even over the evil that men do. Within a few hours, Jesus would be betrayed and sold into the hands of men who would put Him to death. He would be severely beaten, nailed to a cross, and left to die. When it happened, the disciples were not to think something had gone terribly wrong in the eternal plan and purpose of God. All appearances aside, evil had not overthrown righteousness on an eternal, cosmic scale. Rather, the cross was ordained by God for a good and holy purpose.

The context of the Old Testament prophecy Jesus cited is instructive. Psalm 41 has historical as well as prophetic meaning. It is David's lament over his own betrayal by his trusted adviser and friend Ahithophel. David had a wayward son named Absalom, who decided to start a rebellion, overthrow his father, and take over the throne. Ahithophel turned against David and joined Absalom's rebellion. The picture of betrayal Psalm 41 draws from the account of David and Ahithophel is fleshed out and fulfilled in a greater, richer sense by Judas's betrayal of Jesus. The phrase "lifted his heel" portrays brutal violence—the swift raising of a heel that is then used to stomp one's adversary into oblivion. That is a figurative description of what Judas tried to do to Jesus. The already-wounded victim is lying injured on the ground, and the one-time friend raises the heel of his boot and viciously crushes the neck.

Psalm 55 contains a similar prophecy of Judas and his betrayal. Imagine Jesus speaking these words to Judas:

> For it is not an enemy who taunts me—then I could bear it; it is not an adversary who deals insolently with me—then I could hide from him. But it is you, a man, my equal, my companion, my familiar friend. We used to take sweet counsel together; within God's house we walked in the throng . . .
>
> My companion stretched out his hand against his friends; he violated his covenant. His speech was smooth as butter, yet war was in his heart; his words were softer than oil, yet they were drawn swords (vv. 12–14, 20–21).

Zechariah 11:12–13 contains yet another prophecy about the betrayal of Christ by Judas in even more meticulous detail, giving the exact price the traitor was paid for his treachery "Then I said to them,

'If it seems good to you, give me my wages; but if not, keep them.' And they weighed out as my wages thirty pieces of silver. Then the Lord said to me, 'Throw it to the potter'—the lordly price at which I was priced by them. So I took the thirty pieces of silver and threw them into the house of the Lord, to the potter."

That describes to the letter what Judas did after the death of Jesus Christ. He took the thirty pieces right back to the house of the Lord and threw them down. Matthew 27 says the thirty pieces were picked up and used to buy a potter's field—exactly fulfilling the prophecy of Zechariah 11.

So Jesus' choosing Judas was no accident. Long before Judas was ever born, his hatred of Christ was foretold, ordained for a good purpose by God's eternal decree—predestined in the plan of God from eternity past. Jesus made that point over and over. In John 17:12, praying to the Father, He says of the disciples, "While I was with them, I kept them in your name, which you have given me. I have guarded them, and not one of them has been lost except the son of destruction, that the Scripture might be fulfilled."

DIVINE SOVEREIGNTY AND HUMAN CHOICE

To repeat a vitally important point: Judas's sin was not imposed on him. The part he played in the death of Christ was not a role he was forced into apart from his own will. Even though God planned and ordained that Christ would be betrayed by this wayward disciple, Judas's own evil will was the seedbed in which the deed was hatched. He did what he did freely and willingly, by his own wicked choice. Judas was no robot. God did not simply allocate to an unwilling Judas the part of the villain in the crucifixion. Such a thing would be inconsistent with the character and purpose of God, who "cannot be tempted with evil, and he himself tempts no one" (James 1:13). It would likewise be inconsistent with the spirit of Christ, who wept over Jerusalem because of the unbelief there, "saying, 'Would that you, even you, had known on this day the things that make for peace!'" (Luke 19:42). Surely He derived no satisfaction from Judas's apostasy. Much less did He sovereignly constrain Judas to commit this gross act of unbelief and treachery against Judas's will.

The notion that Jesus wanted Judas to fail, or that He sovereignly caused him to fail, is also inconsistent with the historical record. During Jesus' ministry, He endeavored to lead Judas to repentance. Judas got the same care, instruction, and advantages that were given to the other eleven disciples. Judas heard every sermon; he was privy to every private session the twelve spent with Jesus; and he was favored with the privilege of belonging to Christ's inner circle of fellowship. Furthermore, all Jesus' pleas for repentance, His calls to faith, His proposals of mercy, and His rebukes were every bit as applicable to Judas as they were any other listener. He was blessed with unspeakable privileges, and he squandered them all.

So although Judas's betrayal of Christ fit perfectly into the eternal plan of God, God was not the efficient cause or the author of Judas's treachery. God did not make him evil, or compel him to sin. Judas became a traitor to Christ by his own choice. God merely took Judas, wretched and treacherous as he was, and used his evil act for eternal good.

Consider this: if God were responsible for making Judas what he was, Jesus would have pitied him rather than rebuking him. Judas Iscariot, then, in accord with his own will, was the chosen instrument of God to betray Christ and thereby bring about His death. God, in accord with His perfect will, His consummate righteousness, and His inscrutable wisdom, used that horrific evil to accomplish an infinite good. Thus God turned Judas's wickedness, and the Devil's evil intentions, on their head, to the glory of His everlasting grace.

Walking with Jesus but Following Satan

Through his treachery, Judas supplies sinners with a solemn warning. We learn from his example that a person can be very near to Jesus Christ and yet be lost and damned forever. Nobody was ever closer to Christ than the twelve. Judas was one of them, but he is nevertheless in hell today. While he may have given intellectual assent to the truth, he never embraced Christ with heartfelt faith.

Judas wasn't deceived; he was a phony. He understood the truth, and he posed as a believer. Furthermore, he was good at what he did—the cleverest hypocrite we read about in all the Scriptures, for no one ever suspected him. He had everyone completely fooled except Jesus, who knew his heart.

Wherever God's work is done, there are impostors like Judas. There will always be hypocrites among the brethren. The favorite trick of Satan and those he employs is to "disguise themselves as servants of righteousness" (2 Corinthians 11:15). Like Judas, "such men are false apostles, deceitful workmen, disguising themselves as apostles of Christ. And no wonder, for even Satan disguises himself as an angel of light" (vv. 13–14). The Devil himself is a master at making his work look good—and he is busily at work among the Lord's people.

Truth and Consequences

Prior to the last Passover meal with His disciples, Jesus had maintained complete secrecy about Judas's hypocrisy. Now He was determined to reveal the truth. As we noted previously, He knew that if Judas's betrayal took the other eleven disciples by complete surprise, their faith might be undermined. Jesus wanted them to know that He was not unaware of what was about to happen. God is never any man's victim, and this would be no exception. Revealing to them what He knew in advance would strengthen the disciples' faith, helping to ensure that when He was gone, they would remain strong and steadfast.

In unmasking Judas, Jesus also irrefutably affirmed His deity. In John 13:19, He says, "I am telling you this now, before it takes place, that when it does take place you may believe that I am he." The "he" in that verse is not in the original Greek text, and the significance of Jesus' statement is expressed more clearly without it. "I am" is of course, the name by which God revealed Himself to Moses (cf. Exodus 3:14). Jesus was taking the name of God for Himself. He was in essence saying, "I want you to know that I am *God*. I know Judas's heart, and I know everything that is about to happen."

Thus with the simple statement of verse 19, He affirmed His name and established His omniscience. Nothing is hidden from His sight. He knows what goes on in Christians' hearts, but more than that, He knows what goes on in the hearts of unregenerate people as well. In John 5:42, speaking to unbelieving Jews, Jesus says, "I know that you do not have the love of God within you." He knows the heart of every person, believers and unbelievers alike, and He reads them like open books.

THE APOSTLES AND THE BETRAYER

In John 13:20, after affirming His deity—still speaking of His imminent betrayal—Jesus says, "Truly, truly, I say to you, whoever receives the one I send receives me, and whoever receives me receives the one who sent me." Initially, that statement seems out of place in this portion of the narrative. But a closer look reveals that it fits the context beautifully.

We don't know what occurred during the gap between verses 19 and 20. But it is easy to imagine that, when the disciples found out about the betrayal, they all assumed that because of the failure of one of their own inner circle, the credibility of the other eleven would be completely destroyed. They might have assumed that a traitor among them would surely lower the standing of the rest. The death of Jesus—so publicly and ignominiously on a cross, no less—would only further discredit all of them. They surely assumed that if Jesus went to the cross, all messianic hope would be gone. Their ministry would be over. They might as well forget about the kingdom. And since Jesus had just been stressing the importance of humility, the disciples might have thought He was telling them to forget about their high calling.

What Jesus was actually saying is this: "No matter what happens, it doesn't lower your commission, and it doesn't alter your calling. You are still My sent ones—*My* ambassadors and representatives. Although there's a traitor among you, that doesn't affect your high calling. The treachery of Judas must never lower your estimate of apostolic responsibility." It was a tremendous lesson for them. He's saying, "When you go out there and preach, if they receive you they are receiving Me. And if they receive Me, they are receiving the Father who sent Me. Your commission is that high. You represent God in the world."

Christ would indeed be crucified. Judas would turn out to be a despicable hypocrite. The whole world would seem to be collapsing. The disciples would hit rock bottom spiritually and emotionally. Jesus knew what was coming, so He took the opportunity there in the upper room to prepare them, elevate them, and encourage them to keep their focus where it belonged—on their calling, and on the ministry Christ had trained and commissioned them for.

We need to be aware of that truth as well. No matter what satanic opposition we run into, no matter how frustrating the obstacles and disappointments in our ministry become, nothing can lower our commission. I frequently encounter people who have become discouraged in the Lord's service. Young pastors in particular seem to face so much opposition that they often wonder if they are even fit for ministry. I always remind them that opposition is to be expected. Anything we do for God is going to be resisted by the powers of evil. If every missionary looked at a mission field and said, "Oh, they might not believe me over there," the church would never get anything done. Just because the work is difficult, and just because we meet with adversity, that cannot alter our calling. We are Christ's ambassadors to the world. Those who reject us reject Christ. Regardless of what happens, we ought to hold firm and persevere with Him. There is no higher ground on which to stand.

When a believer carries the gospel of Christ into this world, he represents Jesus Christ. Paul says in 2 Corinthians 5:20, "We are ambassadors for Christ, God making his appeal through us. We implore you on behalf of Christ, be reconciled to God." In Galatians 4:14, the apostle Paul says, "You did not scorn or despise me, but received me as an angel of God, as Christ Jesus." And that's the way everyone ought to receive a believer. When a person rejects our witness for Christ, he rejects Jesus the Son and God the Father. That's how strategically important believers are. And that's Jesus' point in John 13:20. Notice the word "whoever." In the original language the indefinite pronoun is paired with a Greek particle that accents the "whosoever" sense of the pronoun. It is a reference to Christ's ambassadors from every tongue, tribe, and nation; from every age, every social class; from every vocation and every walk of life. It categorically includes those of us who represent Him today.

Have you ever heard someone use the existence of hypocrites in the church as an excuse for not following Christ? People often say, "There are too many hypocrites in the church for me." Or, "Well, we don't go to church because we went when I was nine and we saw a hypocrite. Haven't been back in forty-two years!" That will be a pathetic excuse when they present it to God at the judgment seat.

It is true that there are too many hypocrites in the church. They're everywhere. And one hypocrite is one too many. But the fact that some are hypocrites does not diminish the glory of God or lower the high calling of every true child of God. One betrayer among the apostles did not tarnish the calling of the rest.

WHEAT AND TARES

In Matthew 13:24–30, Jesus gives this parable:

> The kingdom of heaven may be compared to a man who sowed good seed in his field, but while his men were sleeping, his enemy came and sowed weeds among the wheat and went away. So when the plants came up and bore grain, then the weeds appeared also.
>
> And the servants of the master of the house came and said to him, "Master, did you not sow good seed in your field? How then does it have weeds?"
>
> He said to them, "An enemy has done this."
>
> So the servants said to him, "Then do you want us to go and gather them?"
>
> But he said, "No, lest in gathering the weeds you root up the wheat along with them. Let both grow together until the harvest, and at harvest time I will tell the reapers, Gather the weeds first and bind them in bundles to be burned, but gather the wheat into my barn."

In other words, it was hard to tell the difference between wheat and tares before everything was ready for harvest. And although there may be some telltale signs, we can't always accurately discern the difference between the true people of God and the out-and-out hypocrites. If we knew which was which, we could purge the visible church of hypocrisy. But we can't read people's hearts. Someday Jesus is going to reveal who is true and who is false, and He will divide the sheep from the goats accordingly.

THE TROUBLED HEART AND THE HARDENED HEART

Unmasking Judas's betrayal clearly caused deep anguish within the heart of Jesus. "After saying these things, Jesus was troubled in his spirit, and testified, 'Truly, truly, I say to you, one of you will betray me'" (John 13:21).

What troubled Him? Possibly a number of things: His unrequited love for Judas; the hypocrisy of the one about to betray Him; the ingratitude in Judas's heart; the spiritual darkness Jesus knew was about to swallow up Judas and damn him forever. Jesus had a deep loathing for sin, and sitting at the same table with Him was sin incarnate. He knew Judas faced an eternal destiny in hell. It seems He could see with His omnipotent eye Satan moving around Judas. We know that our Lord perfectly understood the exceeding sinfulness of sin; He knew precisely what the awful wages of sin entailed for Judas. Jesus Himself would personally have to bear that burden in its entirety on the cross the very next day. No wonder the Savior was troubled in spirit.

In that state of deep anguish Christ said, "One of you will betray me." Imagine the shock that must have rattled the disciples. Their hearts must have raced when they realized He was accusing one from their inner circle. All of them were there at the table. Someone whose feet Jesus had just washed—someone they all knew and trusted—was about to betray the Master. One of them was plotting to use his intimacy with Christ to help the enemy find their Lord and kill Him. It must have been difficult for them to fathom that one of their own could have such hardened treachery in his heart.

In fact, the disciples couldn't imagine whom Jesus might be talking about. John says, "The disciples looked at one another, uncertain of whom he spoke" (13:22). Matthew says they all sorrowfully said, "Is it I, Lord?" Even Judas, the devious hypocrite himself, said, "Is it I, Rabbi?" (Matthew 26:22, 25).

LOVE AND TREACHERY

It is noteworthy that the disciples were so perplexed. It shows that Jesus had always treated Judas with exactly the same loving-kindness and tenderness that He showed the rest of them. They had all been together about three years. Even though Jesus knew from the beginning that Judas would betray Him, He never treated Judas any differently from the way He treated the others. If He had been more distant or shown any sign of resentment, they would have known immediately that Judas was the betrayer. If Jesus had harbored any bitterness for what He knew Judas would ultimately do, it would have come out in the way He talked to him. But, evidently, for three years He had been gentle, loving, and affectionate to Judas—extending to the traitor every kindness and every privilege that were given the other eleven. They thought of him as a close brother and fellow disciple. No one suspected him of disloyalty.

On the contrary, they must have had an extraordinary amount of trust in him, because Judas was their treasurer. But hard-hearted Judas had just played his game. He had the behavior of a saint and the heart of a total reprobate. He must have loathed Christ deeply.

The hatred of Judas and the love of John make an interesting contrast. Try to picture the scene around their last meal together. The table itself most likely would have been V-shaped. In accordance with the customs of that time, the disciples would not have been seated on chairs, but rather reclining on long, low couches. The table would have been at the same height—a solid block with the couches around it. The host's place was at the center. The places next to him were reserved for honored guests.

Jesus would have occupied that center position when eating with His disciples. On either side of Him would have been His closest disciples. Others would take their places around the table. They would recline on their left sides, resting on their left elbows, using their right hands to eat. Thus the one who was to the right of Jesus would have had his head very close to Christ's heart. From a distance, he would have appeared to be reclining on the Lord's breast.

John, who wrote this account, was in that place of honor. He often referred to himself as "the disciple whom Jesus loved" (John 21:20; cf. v. 24). It was not that Jesus loved him more than the others, but rather that John was completely overwhelmed with the concept that Jesus loved him at all. Also, John was consumed with love for the Lord. He loved Jesus as much as Judas hated him.

John writes: "One of his disciples, whom Jesus loved, was reclining at table close to Jesus, so Simon Peter motioned to him to ask Jesus of whom he was speaking" (John 13:23–24). Peter's suggestion no doubt came as a subtle, silent gesture, unnoticed by anyone else. John tells us he leaned back against Jesus and whispered, "Lord, who is it?" (v. 25).

"Jesus answered, 'It is he to whom I will give this morsel of bread when I have dipped it.' So when He had dipped the morsel, he gave it to Judas, the son of Simon Iscariot" (v. 26). Jesus' answer to Peter and John was actually a gesture of grace to Judas—a final loving appeal for his repentance. The "morsel" was a piece of bread broken from some of the unleavened cakes that were on the table as a part of the Passover feast. Also on the table was a dish called cheshireth. It contained bitter herbs, vinegar, salt, and mashed fruit (consisting of dates, figs, raisins, and a little water)—all blended together into a pasty substance. Jesus and His disciples ate it with the unleavened bread like a dip.

It was a formal display of honor for the host to dip a morsel into the cheshireth and give it to a guest. Jesus, in a kind gesture of love toward Judas, dipped the morsel and handed it to him—as if Judas were a singular guest of honor.

When Jesus told John the morsel signified who would betray Him, He probably whispered, so no one but John heard what He was doing. But after everything Jesus had said about the disciple who would betray Him, Judas undoubtedly understood that Jesus knew full well what he intended to do. The fact that the Lord responded with a simple gesture of honor ought to have broken Judas's heart. ("Do you presume on the riches of his kindness and forbearance and patience, not knowing that God's kindness is meant to lead you to repentance?"—Romans 2:4.) But it didn't. Judas was an apostate. His heart was hardened, and nothing Jesus could do for him would penetrate. Salvation for him was now impossible. He had become the classic example of the kind of person the writer of Hebrews describes: "It is impossible, in the case of those who have once been enlightened, who have tasted the heavenly gift, and have shared in the Holy Spirit, and have tasted the goodness of the word of God and the powers of the age to come, and then have fallen away, to restore them again to repentance, since they are crucifying once again the Son of God to their own harm and holding him up to contempt" (Hebrews 6:4–6).

Judas had seen and experienced and tasted all those things, but he had never embraced them with true faith.

Judas was so confirmed in his apostasy that Satan now literally possessed him. John 13:27 says, "After he had taken the morsel, Satan entered into him. Jesus said to him, 'What you are going to do, do quickly.'" Judas had been flirting with Satan, and now Satan had duped and totally enslaved Judas. The intention was already in Judas's heart to betray Christ. Satan simply moved in and took over. In that dreadful moment, the evil will of Judas rejected the last tender gesture of Jesus Christ's love, and this hard-hearted turncoat's deliberate sin against the Holy Spirit was finalized—forever unforgivable. Judas's damnation was therefore irreversibly sealed. He had spurned the love of Christ for the last time, and the door of divine grace was now fastened shut against him forever.

DAY AND NIGHT

Jesus' attitude toward Judas immediately changed. He was through with Judas. The defector had crossed the line of grace, and Jesus could no longer bear his presence. No more would the Savior reach out to him. The difference was immediate, radical—like day and night. Jesus' dealings with him were now over. Judas was confirmed in stubborn, deliberate apostasy. All Jesus wanted now was to get rid of him.

Notice that Satan and Jesus were now giving Judas the same direction. Satan said. "Betray Him." Christ said, "Do it quickly." Judas was clearly set on betraying his Master. Satan was determined to destroy God's anointed. And Christ was prepared to die for a multitude of sinners. (Jesus would in the end shatter Satan's plan by emerging triumphant from the grave. And Judas would get precisely what he bargained for.)

None of the disciples caught the significance of what was occurring. "No one at the table knew why he said this to him. Some thought that, because Judas had the moneybag, Jesus was telling him, 'Buy what we need for the feast,' or that he should give something to the poor" (John 13:28–29). They thought he was going shopping, or out to dispense some charity at the Passover season.

"So, after receiving the morsel of bread, he immediately went out. And it was night" (v. 30). There he went, a solitary figure leaving the room to enter into the eternal grip of hell. The Bible doesn't say where he went, but evidently he went to finalize his deal with the Sanhedrin. And when he went out, Scripture says, "It was night."

For Judas, who had walked with Jesus and yet stayed in darkness, the hours of daylight and opportunity were over. It was much more than merely the nighttime that comes with literal sundown. It was eternal night in the soul of Judas. It is always night when someone flees from the presence of Jesus Christ.

Judas stands as a classic illustration of the tragic, soul-destroying wretchedness sin produces. Sadly, there are Judases in every age. Perhaps they are more common than ever today. The professing church is full of people willing to sell out Jesus Christ, thus "crucifying once again the Son of God to their own harm and holding him up to contempt" (Hebrews 6:6). There are many who have eaten at His table and then lifted their heel against Him. And the greatest tragedy still is only their own ultimate disaster.

Hester Cholmondeley was an English girl whose young life ended at age 22 in 1892 (the same year Charles Spurgeon died). Only four years earlier, she had begun keeping a journal that ultimately ran to nearly a quarter-million words. Contained in her writings was a short verse about Judas that sums up the tragedy of his life in these few poignant words:

Still as of old,
Man by himself is priced.
For thirty pieces Judas sold
Himself, not Christ.[1]

Be sure you make the most of your opportunities. Be sure you're not a hypocrite. If we learn anything from the life of Judas, it is that the greatest spiritual privileges can be neutralized by unrepentant sinful desires and a commitment to evil priorities. A life that is lived in the face of an unclouded sun may yet end in a night of despair.

---

1 Mary Cholmondeley, *Diana Tempest* (London: Richard Bentley & Son, 1894), 124.

Three

THE MARKS OF THE COMMITTED CHRISTIAN

Historically, Christians have displayed a number of different symbols to mark their identity as believers. Lapel pins, fish-shaped insignia, and neck chains with gold crosses are nothing new. They have been used since the early days of the church age as emblems to signify followers of Christ. In recent years, people have also made badges of identity from such items as bumper stickers, posters, T-shirts, decorated Bibles, and jackets with embroidered insignia. I don't have any argument with such tokens, except that they are totally superficial—not even as deep as the surface to which they are attached.

As a Christian, whether or not you wear a button, display a bumper sticker, or use any other kind of visible symbol is of no real consequence. More important, and infinitely more definitive than all the pins and stickers and buttons, are the internal, spiritual, character-related signs of a true believer.

In John 13:31–38, Jesus gives three distinguishing marks of a committed Christian. With Judas now banished from the ranks of the

45

apostles, Jesus turned to the eleven remaining disciples and gave them a valedictory address.

> When [Judas Iscariot] had gone out, Jesus said, "Now is the Son of Man glorified, and God is glorified in him. If God is glorified in him, God will also glorify him in himself, and glorify him at once. Little children, yet a little while I am with you. You will seek me, and just as I said to the Jews, so now I also say to you, 'Where I am going you cannot come.'
>
> A new commandment I give to you, that you love one another: just as I have loved you, you also are to love one another. By this all people will know that you are my disciples, if you have love for one another."
>
> Simon Peter said to him, "Lord, where are you going?"
>
> Jesus answered him, "Where I am going you cannot follow me now, but you will follow afterward."
>
> Peter said to him, "Lord, why can I not follow you now? I will lay down my life for you."
>
> Jesus answered, "Will you lay down your life for me? Truly, truly, I say to you, the rooster will not crow till you have denied me three times."

That passage introduces Jesus' last commission to His disciples before He went to the cross. His farewell message, which will continue through John 16, contains every ingredient we need to know about discipleship. In fact, the basics of Paul's teaching on the subject seem to match this portion of John. Thus these concluding words of our Lord on His last evening with His disciples are indispensable to knowing what Christ expects of us as believers. The three major characteristics of discipleship Jesus presents should be evident in the life of every believer.

An Unending Preoccupation with the Glory of God

First, the committed Christian is preoccupied with his Lord's glory. The very purpose for which we exist is to give glory to God, so it is right that this is the first mark of a committed Christian. The true believer is not preoccupied with his own glory. He's not worried about what brings honor or recognition to himself. He's not on a popularity binge. He's not trying to climb the ladder to get something bigger and better for himself. He realizes that it doesn't matter how impressed people are with him, but only that they glorify God. His goal is for his own life to reflect the attributes of God, and he wants God to be praised by the way he lives.

Jesus taught His disciples that perspective both by example and by precept: "When he had gone out, Jesus said, 'Now is the Son of Man glorified, and God is glorified in him. If God is glorified in him, God will also glorify him in himself, and glorify him at once. Little children, yet a little while I am with you. You will seek me, and just as I said to the Jews, so now I also say to you, "Where I am going you cannot come"'" (John 13:31–33).

The first phrase of our Lord's statement indicates almost a sense of relief. Now that Judas was gone, He could speak freely to His disciples. God incarnate, Jesus Christ, had come to earth in humility. He had voluntarily restricted the full manifestation of His glory and subjected Himself to human frailty. He Himself never sinned, but He fully experienced every nonsinful expression of human weakness: pain, hunger, thirst, fatigue, and all the inconveniences and indignities of life in a sin-cursed world.

For thirty-three years His glory had been shrouded in human flesh. Before long He would be in His glory again. All the attributes of God would again be fully on display in Him, without restraint and without limits. The process that would culminate in the full recovery of His heavenly glory would begin for Him the very next day. His hour at last had come.

But the road to glory would begin in the most unlikely place—at Calvary, as Christ gave His life on a cross, suffering in the place of sinners.

Still, it was the glory, not the suffering, that Jesus first spoke of. He made three distinct statements. Each is unique and important for us to understand:

"Now is the Son of Man glorified"

The first is in verse 31, a great statement of anticipation: "Now is the Son of Man glorified." Judas had begun to set everything in motion. The Jews had already paid the wretched traitor for his betrayal, and he was now outside, getting everything set. Shortly, Jesus and the disciples would leave the upper room. Christ would continue His teaching as they walked to Gethsemane to pray. There in the garden, while Jesus communed with the Father, Judas would march up to Him with Roman soldiers and set in motion the events that would lead to Jesus' death.

Jesus was prepared to die, and He knew that even though the cross looked like shame, disgrace, and disaster, it signified glory. At first it may seem difficult to understand what dying has to do with glory—especially death by crucifixion. In His death our Lord experienced the deepest kind of indignity, humiliation, accusation, insults, infamy, mockery, spitting, and all the abuse that men could throw at Him. It was the polar opposite of glory. He died hanging between thieves, receiving not only the pain and ignominy of the cross—but more importantly, bearing the full weight of God's wrath against sin.

Yet *knowing* He was facing all that, Jesus could say, "Now is the Son of Man glorified."

Was there really glory in the cross? Yes, because on it Jesus performed the greatest work in the history of the universe. In His death He redeemed lost sinners, destroyed sin, and defeated Satan. He paid the price of sin God's justice demanded, and purchased for Himself all the elect of God. In dying for sin, He rendered His life a sweet-smelling savor to God, a sacrifice more pure and blessed than any ever offered. And when the sacrifice was completed, Jesus declared, "It is finished." He had accomplished the work of atonement He came to do. He had fully satisfied the justice of God. He had fulfilled every aspect of God's law to perfection. And He had bought freedom for all who by faith embrace His glorious work. In all heaven and earth, no act is so worthy of praise, honor, and full glory. (For a thorough treatment of the significance and drama of Christ's death, see John MacArthur, *The Murder of Jesus* [Nashville: Word, 2000].)

"And God is glorified in Him"

Jesus made a second vital statement about glory. Not only was He glorified, but God was glorified in Him. God is glorified through the details of the gospel. When Jesus said, "Now is the Son of Man glorified, and God is glorified in him" (v. 31), He was speaking inclusively of the whole series of redemptive events that would culminate in His eternal glorification: His death, burial, resurrection, exaltation, and coming again. All those events encompass the totality of Christ's perfect glory and the glory of God's redemptive plan. God is therefore glorified in the proclamation of the gospel.

One of the greatest ways we can glorify God is to declare the gospel message—especially to those who have not yet heard. The good news of salvation radiates the glory of God like nothing else in all the universe. In a sense, therefore, witnessing is one of the highest and purest forms of worship.

God's glory is wrapped up in His attributes—His love, mercy, grace, wisdom, omniscience, omnipotence, omnipresence, and so on. All those stunning perfections reflect and declare His glory. We worship and glorify God when we in any way praise, acknowledge, experience, or display His attributes. When we exemplify His love, for instance, we glorify Him. When we acknowledge and yield to His sovereignty, we glorify Him. When we proclaim His greatness to the world, it glorifies Him.

At the cross, every attribute of God was manifest in a way not seen before. The power of God, for example, was made visible there. "The kings of the earth set themselves, and the rulers were gathered together, against the Lord and against his Anointed" (Acts 4:26). The terrible enmity of the carnal mind and the desperate wickedness of the human heart nailed Jesus to a cross. The fiendish hatred of Satan put forth its best effort. The world, the Devil, and every demon in the universe threw all the power they had at Christ, yet He had more than enough power to overcome it all. In death He broke every fleshly form of bondage, every shackle of sin, and every power of Satan forever. His graphic display of God's power thus brought glory to God.

The cross revealed *the justice of God* in all its fullness. "The wages of sin is death" (Romans 6:23), and in order for God to redeem sinners (without nullifying or ignoring the law's righteous requirement), someone had to receive the wages in full. The penalty of the law had to be enforced. Isaiah says that as Jesus hung there on the cross, "the Lord . . . laid on him the iniquity of us all" (Isaiah 53:6). God would not neglect justice, even if it meant the slaying of His beloved Son. Consider this: if every member of the human race were to suffer in hell forever, all their anguish, all the divine wrath poured out on them would still not be enough to atone for sin. What Christ suffered alone was sufficient to pay the price in full on behalf of everyone who will ever believe. Christ glorified God on the cross by fulfilling the requirements of divine justice and thereby upholding the righteousness of God, no matter what the cost.

God's holiness was also manifest at the cross. Habakkuk wrote that God is "of purer eyes than to see evil and cannot look at wrong" (Habakkuk 1:13). Never did God so manifest His hatred for sin as in the suffering and death of His own Son. As Christ suffered on the cross, bearing the sins of the world, God turned away from His only begotten Son. That's why Jesus cried out in agony. "'*Eli, Eli, lema sabachthani?*' that is, 'My God, my God, why have you forsaken me?'" (Matthew 27:46). Even though the Father loved Jesus Christ with an infinite love, His holiness could not tolerate looking with favor on the One who bore the sin of the world. All the cheerful obedience of godly people from every era is nothing compared to the offering of Christ Himself to satisfy every demand of God's holiness. Through that offering, God was glorified.

God's faithfulness also was displayed at the cross. He had promised the world a Savior from the beginning. When Christ, the sinless One, was offered on the cross to receive the full and final wages of sin, God showed to all heaven and earth that He was faithful. Even though it cost Him His only Son, He went through with it. When we see that kind of faithfulness, we are seeing His glory.

Many other attributes of God were displayed in their fullness at the cross, but the one that stands above all the others is the perfection of divine love. "In this is love, not that we have loved God but that he loved us and sent his Son to be the propitiation for our sins" (1 John 4:10). The human mind cannot comprehend the love that would cause God to have His Son die as an atonement for our sins. Frankly, unsanctified intellects often recoil at the thought that the bar of justice is set so high, and that someone so perfect would be permitted to die for others' sins. But God is glorified beyond words and beyond comprehension in the display of such love.

"God will also glorify Him in Himself, and glorify Him at once"

In His third and final statement about glory, Jesus emphasizes the truth that the Father and the Son are busily engaged in glorifying each other. But the greatest glory of the Son will follow His work on the cross. "If God is glorified in him, God will also glorify him in himself, and glorify him at once" (John 13:32). There was a sublime glory in the cross, and it is both profound and far-reaching. As we have seen, it is a glory beyond human comprehension. But the Father would not stop there. The resurrection, the ascension, the exaltation of Christ at the right hand of the Father, and His return in triumphant glory are all important aspects of the glory that would be His. In the final judgment, Christ will be glorified yet again. That means even today, His greatest glory is yet future.

The promise of future glory for Christ meant that (as far as His physical presence was concerned) He had to leave the disciples. Therefore He said, "Little children, yet a little while I am with you. You will seek me, and just as I said to the Jews, so now I also say to you, 'Where I am going you cannot come'" (v. 33). While His thoughts were on future glory and the grandeur of it, He was also thinking about His eleven beloved disciples. He called them "little children"—an expression He probably would not have used if Judas had still been present.

What did He mean, "just as I said to the Jews"? He had once told a group of key Jewish leaders (Pharisees and chief priests) who sought to arrest Him, "I will be with you a little longer, and then I am going to him who sent me. You will seek me and you will not find me. Where I am you cannot come" (John 7:34). John 8:21 says, "He said to them again, 'I am going away, and you will seek me, and you will die in your sin. Where I am going, you cannot come.'" In verses 23–24 He adds, "You are from below; I am from above. You are of this world; I am not of this world. I told you that you would die in your sins, for unless you believe that I am he, you will die in your sins."

It is significant that Jesus gave no such warning to His believing disciples. Although when He ascended they would not be able to follow Him where He was going, there was no danger they would die in their sins. Jesus was going to the Father, and they would miss His physical nearness, especially in times of trial and problems. In fact, as Jesus ascended into heaven, the book of Acts tells us they just stood there, gazing longingly into heaven. They didn't want Him to leave and Jesus knew that, so in John 13 He is reassuring them that although His glory would involve His leaving, He still cared for them. It is the introduction of a theme that will become a unifying motif running through the next few chapters of John's gospel.

Why did Jesus tell the disciples all this? Because He knew that as true disciples, beneath the surface of their immediate fears and confusion, their deepest concern was for His glory. He wanted them to share the anticipation and the excitement of His coming exaltation. He wanted them to be preoccupied with thoughts of His glory.

A concern for God's glory, then, is one of the marks of a true disciple. It is the heart of the reason for our existence. It is a burning passion we inherit from our Lord Himself.

Henry Martyn was one of the great pioneer missionaries to India and Persia. A year before leaving for the mission field, he wrote in his diary, "In morning prayer had a solemn season of reverence and submission to God. I seemed to have no wish in my heart, but that God may be glorified; as it was a comfort to me to reflect, that He will be glorified."[1]

As Martyn made his journey by ship to India, he wrote, "I can scarce picture to myself any greater enjoyment in heaven, than seeing God glorified."[2] A few days later, in reflection, he wrote, "I have hitherto lived to little purpose, more like a clod than a servant of God; now let me burn out for God."[3]

While ministering in a Hindu region, Martyn witnessed the famous festival for the god Jagannath. Thousands of people prostrated themselves before an image drawn on a cart in a frenzy of superstitious passion. Martyn wrote in his diary, "This excited more horror in me than I can well express."[4] On another occasion, he heard a Muslim speak disparagingly of Christ. He wrote,

> I was cut to the soul at this blasphemy. In prayer I could think of nothing else but that great day when the Son of God should come in the clouds of heaven . . . Mirza Seid Ali perceived that I was considerably disordered, and was sorry for having repeated the verse, but asked what it was that was so offensive? I told him, *"I could not endure existence, if Jesus was not glorified; that it would be hell to me, if he were to be always thus dishonoured."*[5]

Asked why he was so preoccupied with Christ's glory, Martyn answered, "If any one pluck out your eyes . . . there is no saying why

---

1 Henry Martyn, *Journal and Letters of Henry Martyn* (New York: Protestant Episcopal Society for the Promotion of Evangelical Knowledge, 1851), 179.

2 Ibid., 312.

3 Ibid., 330.

4 Ibid., 340.

5 John Sargent, *Memoir of the Rev. Henry Martyn, B. D.* (London: Hatchard, 1819), 438–39 (emphasis added).

you feel pain—it is feeling. It is because I am one with Christ that I am thus dreadfully wounded."[6]

Martyn summed up his view of God and the world with these poignant words: "I want to have nothing to do with the world. May I ever remain free and disentangled, pursuing my way unnoticed through the wilderness, finding all my pleasure in secret communion with God, and in seeing Him glorified!"[7]

Every genuine disciple knows something of that feeling. Few of us express it so well or ponder it as carefully as we should.

AN UNFAILING LOVE
FOR THE CHILDREN OF GOD

Not only is the committed disciple preoccupied with his Lord's glory, he also is filled with Christ's love. Perhaps this mark of the committed Christian is the most significant of all in terms of practical living that distinguishes us in the world.

Even though the apostles would no longer be able to rejoice in the visible presence of Jesus, they still would enjoy a full, rich experience of love, for they would have a depository of love in their own lives. In fact, love would be their primary distinguishing mark: "A new commandment I give to you, that you love one another: just as I have loved you, you also are to love one another. By this all people will know that you are my disciples, if you have love for one another" (John 13:34–35). Those words of Christ had such a profound impact on the apostle John that he made them his life's message: "This is the message that you have heard from the beginning, that we should love one another" (1 John 3:11).

6 Ibid., 439.
7 Martyn, *Journal and Letters*, 305.

As believers in Christ, we have a new God-given capacity to love, "because God's love has been poured into our hearts through the Holy Spirit who has been given to us" (Romans 5:5).

We also therefore have a new relationship with the law of God, because love perfectly fulfills the law's moral demands:

Owe no one anything, except to love each other, for the one who loves another has fulfilled the law. For the commandments, "You shall not commit adultery, You shall not murder, You shall not steal, You shall not covet," and any other commandment, are summed up in this word: "You shall love your neighbor as yourself." Love does no wrong to a neighbor; therefore love is the fulfilling of the law. (Romans 13:8–10)

"The whole law is fulfilled in one word: 'You shall love your neighbor as yourself'" (Galatians 5:14). "Love . . . binds everything together in perfect harmony" (Colossians 3:14).

In other words, the one who truly loves embraces the duties of the law willingly, not under compulsion. To illustrate: we don't need signs or law-enforcement officers in our houses saying, "Don't pistol-whip your wife"; "Don't bash your children with a hammer." Likewise, those who genuinely love their neighbors won't steal, kill, or bear false witness, either. To violate those commandments is to fail in the duty of love. Love, then, is what the moral precepts of God's law are all about (cf. Matthew 22:40). James referred to the Second Great Commandment ("You shall love your neighbor as yourself") as "the royal law" (James 2:8).

When David wrote, "Oh how I love your law!" (Psalm 119:97), he was not talking about the law's penalty, or the fact that it condemns sinners, "For the law brings wrath" (Romans 4:15). He was certainly not commending the law as a means of salvation for sinners, "For all who rely on works of the law are under a curse" (Galatians 3:10). He was affirming the same thing the apostle Paul wrote in Roman 7:12: "The law is holy, and the commandment is holy and righteous and good." David was writing as a believer, a forgiven man, who sees the excellence of the law's moral standard. Of course, he loved the law! Boil down the law to its bare moral essence, and it is all about love. It is significant, too, that the law was perfectly fulfilled by no one other than Christ, whose love is as perfect as His righteousness. Indeed, those two ideas (perfect love and perfect righteousness) are inextricably bound together. Therefore, inherent in all genuine, Christlike love is a love for everything the law teaches us. That's precisely what David was expressing.

What else does the Bible say about the love that distinguishes a true disciple? Note from what we have said that love is not at all what the world thinks it is. It isn't merely a kind of easygoing tolerance of every idea and opinion. It's not defined by what is politically correct. It's not the same thing as romance. It's not merely a feeling that happens to us. In fact, it's not a feeling at all. It is *a commitment to the good of others, and a willingness to sacrifice for their sake.* "Greater love has no one than this, that someone lay down his life for his friends" (John 15:13).

Furthermore, Jesus says, "Love one another as I have loved you." That sets the standard extremely high. Jesus' love is holy, selfless, sacrificial, gracious, unconditional, understanding, and forgiving. Unless your love is like that, you have not fulfilled the new commandment.

And let's face it: none of us has truly fulfilled it. We are sinners, so we will never attain such perfection until we are glorified. Still, that is precisely the goal toward which we must press. As Paul said, "Not that I have already obtained this or am already perfect, but I press on to make it my own, because Christ Jesus has made me his own" (Philippians 3:12). If Christians would simply *pursue* Christlike love with any degree of earnestness, we would absolutely overwhelm the world.

Unfortunately, that isn't the way the professing church operates. There are factions, splits, and cliques. Churchgoers gossip, backbite, talk too much, and criticize. People in the world look and they don't see much love. So there is no way for them to know whether those who call themselves Christians are real or not.

One reason pseudo-Christian cults and false doctrines have so much influence today is that not many Christians are fully devoted disciples, earnestly seeking to exhibit the love of Christ to one another. Worldly affections, hostile to true Christlike love, have infiltrated the church. People who claim to be Christians tend to be as superficial and self-absorbed as anyone else. There's a lot of talk nowadays about "love," but the visible church is much too influenced by corrupt, worldly notions of what true love is. We do not cultivate and exemplify that distinctive, Christlike, holy love that Jesus commanded His disciples to be characterized by.

The average church is too obsessed with impressing the world by imitating worldly styles to be distinctive—even when it comes to the quality and character of our love for one another. It's no wonder the church's testimony to the world is so ineffective. The average person looks at the spectrum of "Christianity" and all that goes with it, and finds it utterly baffling. Those who claim to be Christians seem to have no distinguishing marks. Even the most biblically ignorant pagan can see the hypocrisy of Christians whose values are worldly, egocentric, and frivolous. That sort of hypocrisy is the very antithesis of authentic love, and the world understands that, even if many in the church are blind to it.

Earlier in John 13, as we've already discussed in chapter 1 of our study, Jesus taught the disciples by washing their feet that the key to love is humility. Here is how closely love is tied to humility: If your love is not what it ought to be, it's because of pride. God hates a proud heart. Those whose hearts are totally given over to pride have no capacity for love at all. But even regenerate people struggle with the remnants of sinful pride. Pride is fleshly and therefore must be mortified. Where it is permitted to dwell, it is destructive to authentic love.

In Philippians 2:3–4, Paul says. "Do nothing from rivalry or conceit, but in humility count others more significant than yourselves. Let each of you look not only to his own interests, but also to the interests of others." That is exactly what Jesus did, and that's how He taught His disciples to love.

How can we manifest visible love? First, we can admit it when we have wronged someone. If you are not willing to go to someone you have wronged and make things right, you call into question your commitment to Christ, and the church will suffer because of your unwillingness to love. Most of the bitterness within the visible church has nothing to do with doctrinal differences. It derives instead from a fundamental lack of love and an unwillingness to accept the humility that love demands.

A second way to show love is by forgiving those who have wronged us—whether we are asked or not. No matter how serious the wrong you have suffered may be, love demands that you forgive it. Christ prayed for forgiveness for those who had mocked Him, spit on Him, and then crucified Him (Luke 23:34). He prayed that prayer while He hung on the cross, at the height of His torment—while the soldiers who nailed Him there were still poking fun at Him (v. 36). The wrongs we generally suffer seem insignificant compared to what He suffered, and yet how willing are we to follow His example and forgive immediately?

Scripture is clear and unyielding on this principle of unconditional forgiveness. First Corinthians 6:1 says, "When one of you has a grievance against another, does he dare go to law before the unrighteous instead of the saints?" (Some of the Corinthians were apparently suing other believers in secular courts!) Verse 7 says, "To have lawsuits at all with one another is already a defeat for you. Why not rather suffer wrong? Why not rather be defrauded?" No verse in all of Scripture is more practical and demanding than that.

Do you really want to maintain a testimony of love in this world? Then accept whatever comes your way, praise the Lord, and let His love flow through you to the one who wronged you. That kind of love would confound this world.

Real love is costly, and the one who truly loves will have to sacrifice. But while you sacrifice in this world you're gaining immeasurably in the spiritual realm. And you are displaying the most visible, practical, obvious mark of a true disciple.

An Unswerving Loyalty to the Son of God

A third mark of the committed Christian is loyalty. It is more implied than expressed in the context of John 13. Nevertheless, loyalty is included with a marvelous illustration from the experience of Peter. He faltered and embarrassed himself often, and one of his most monumental failures occurred on this very night. But ultimately he proved himself to be a true disciple. From him we learn a number of intensely practical principles about true devotion and unswerving loyalty to Christ.

One clear lesson is that discipleship demands more than a *promised* loyalty. We must go beyond making vows to God (which we tend to do all too glibly). Discipleship demands a *practiced* loyalty—an operating, functioning, persistent loyalty that holds up under every kind of pressure. Loyalty that is easily derailed is no loyalty at all. That's called fickleness.

All this talk about Jesus' going away must have deeply bothered Peter. He couldn't stand the thought of Jesus' leaving. Matthew 16:22 vividly shows how intensely Peter hated the thought of Jesus' impending death. Jesus had foretold His crucifixion and resurrection, and Peter, always the self-appointed spokesman for the disciples, took Jesus aside "and began to rebuke him, saying, 'Far be it from you, Lord! This shall never happen to you.'" This was a stubborn, selfish attitude from Peter, who did not want Jesus to be taken from him under any conditions. Jesus "turned and said to Peter, 'Get behind me, Satan! You are a hindrance to me. For you are not setting your mind on the things of God, but on the things of man'" (v. 23).

Jesus was completely aware of Peter's attitude, and that night at supper, He took the opportunity to teach Peter a lesson about true loyalty. When Jesus said, "Where I am going you cannot come" (John 13:33), it was predictable that Peter would speak up. This time he was somewhat more cautious—at least he started out that way:

> Simon Peter said to him, "Lord, where are you going?"
>
> Jesus answered him, "Where I am going you cannot follow me now, but you will follow afterward."
>
> Peter said to him, "Lord, why can I not follow you now? I will lay down my life for you."
>
> Jesus answered, "Will you lay down your life for me? Truly, truly, I say to you, the rooster will not crow till you have denied me three times." (John 13:36–38)

Peter's heart was burning with love for Jesus. But while his love for Jesus was admirable, his boasting was foolish. His refusal to accept Jesus' words was an expression of stubborn pride. In essence, he was saying, "If all You're going to do is die, I will be happy to die with You." But he was speaking rashly, as a braggart. Perhaps he said it for the benefit of the other disciples. Maybe he thought he could rouse courage in all of them. But he was saying it in the flesh. Worst of all, the message to Jesus was, "I know better than You."

You can imagine what a shock it was to Peter when Jesus predicted that he would deny Him that very night. In fact, through the rest of the dialogue, Peter—uncharacteristically—never said another word.

Nevertheless, Matthew 26:31 reports that later that evening, on the way to Gethsemane, Jesus told the disciples, "You will all fall away because of me this night. For it is written, 'I will strike the shepherd, and the sheep of the flock will be scattered.'"

Peter repeated his boast again: "Though they all fall away because of you, I will never fall away" (v. 33).

"Jesus said to him, 'Truly, I tell you, this very night, before the rooster crows, you will deny me three times'" (v. 34).

Peter, still in an argumentative frame of mind, "said to him, 'Even if I must die with you, I will not deny you!'" (v. 35). This time, "all the disciples said the same" (v. 35).

But within the hour, with their lives truly on the line, "All the disciples forsook him and fled" (v. 56). There was a huge gap between their promise and their practice when their loyalty was truly put to the test. Peter, who had so loudly boasted that he would stand by the Lord no matter what, failed miserably. Instead of giving his life for Jesus, he tried to save it by denying Him. And he didn't do it in silence or by implication. He did it loudly with cursing—before many witnesses.

Four things made Peter fail the test of loyalty.

He Boasted Too Much

First, Peter was too proud to listen to what Jesus was trying to tell him. And he was too busy boasting. Luke 22:31–32 records Jesus' admonition to Peter: "Simon, Simon, behold, Satan demanded to have you, that he might sift you like wheat, but I have prayed for you that your faith may not fail. And when you have turned again, strengthen your brothers." Implied in that warning is the prophecy that Peter *would* fail. Also understood was the fact that he would later repent of his failure.

But Peter missed the whole point. "Lord, I am ready to go with you both to prison and to death" (v. 33). First Kings 20:11 includes this wise Hebrew saying: "Let not him who straps on his armor boast himself as he who takes it off." Peter was boasting in his flesh, but he wasn't in a position to boast about anything.

He Prayed Too Little

Peter also failed because his praying was not what it should have been. First, he was boasting while he should have been listening, and later that evening, he slept when he should have been praying. Sleep is a good thing, but it's not a substitute for prayer. While Jesus was praying in agony in Gethsemane, Peter and the other disciples fell asleep. Luke 22:40, 45–46 records this scene in the garden: "When [Jesus] came to the place, he said to them, 'Pray that you may not enter into temptation.' . . . [But later,] when he rose from prayer, he came to the disciples and found them sleeping for sorrow, and he said to them, 'Why are you sleeping? Rise and pray that you may not enter into temptation.'"

That rebuke must have made a profound impact on Peter, for many years later he wrote, "Be self-controlled and sober-minded for the sake of your prayers" (1 Peter 4:7). The Greek expression translated "be . . . sober-minded" means "watch; stay alert." That is not some kind of abstract theological reasoning; Peter is talking out of his own life.

He Acted Too Fast

Another reason Peter failed the test of loyalty is that he was impetuous. Acting without thinking was a perennial problem in Peter's life. When a group of officers from the priests and Pharisees came into the garden to take Jesus, Peter grabbed a sword and cut off the high priest's slave's ear (Luke 22:50). (This was not a surgical strike. Peter no doubt intended to split the man's head open, but he missed.) His motive wasn't noble. This was an act of selfishness—or perhaps fear or pride—but not loyalty. Jesus rebuked him for his action and healed the man's ear.

God's will is not always easy to accept, but those who are truly loyal will be sensitive to discern it. Peter might have thought he was helping the cause of God, but he was totally oblivious to all that God was doing in Jesus' sufferings and death, and his impetuous actions actually were getting in God's way and leading to his own failure.

He Followed Too Far Away

A final reason for Peter's great failure is that he left Jesus' side and began to follow from a distance. Luke 22:54 says, "They seized him and led him away, bringing him into the high priest's house, and Peter was following at a distance." It's good that he was following Jesus at all. He was alone in that. "All [the others] left him and fled" (Mark 14:50). But Peter wasn't doing as he had promised. He wasn't fulfilling his boast. And as he kept his distance to avoid being discovered, disaster loomed on the horizon.

Here was the logical consequence of all of Peter's weaknesses: *cowardice.* He had foolishly boasted of his willingness to die; now when he had that opportunity, Peter, for the first time in their relationship, drifted from his rightful place near Jesus.

"And when they had kindled a fire in the middle of the courtyard and sat down together, Peter sat down among them" (Luke 22:55). Suddenly he was sitting in the seat of the scornful. Verse 56 states that a servant girl recognized him as a follower of Jesus and pointed him out. Peter, who had bragged so forcefully about his loyalty, now began to deny even more forcefully that he had ever known Jesus.

There he was, keeping his distance but within sight of the Lord, denying Him, even cursing and swearing that he had never known Him (Matthew 26:72). When the rooster crowed, Jesus turned around and looked at Peter (Luke 22:61), and Peter remembered. He was so ashamed that all he could do was run away and cry his heart out (v. 62).

What about your loyalty? What promises have you made to Jesus? That you would love Him? That you would serve Him? That you would be faithful, always affirm Him, forsake sin, live or die for Him, witness to your neighbor?

How have you done? Did you boast too much? Pray too little? Act too fast? Follow too far away? All of the above?

It wasn't too late for Peter, and it is not too late for you. Peter finally passed the test of loyalty. In the end, he *did* preach, suffer, and die for his Lord, just as he had promised. He proved himself to be a genuine disciple. The first part of his story may be sad, but beginning with the book of Acts we begin to see a different Peter.

Perhaps this is the most significant thing we learn from Peter: God can turn a life around when it is finally humbled, chastened, and truly yielded to Him. What kind of a Christian are you? Are you everything you promised Jesus Christ you would be when you first believed? How are you doing in the work of fulfilling the promises you made more recently? Are there visible, distinguishing marks that show you are a deeply committed believer?

You may lack the marks of a committed Christian, but God will forgive your failure. His grace can also transform you into a true disciple if you trust and surrender to Him rather than trusting your own flesh. The life of faith is contrary to our natural instincts, and it may be costly, but it is the only kind of life that really counts for eternity.

Four

———⋙⋘———

THE SOLUTION TO A TROUBLED HEART

Those were dark hours that night before the Lord was betrayed, abused, tortured, and ultimately crucified. In a very short time the world of the eleven disciples was going to collapse into unbelievable chaos. Jesus, for whom they had forsaken all, was leaving. Their beloved Master, whom they loved more than life, the One whom they had been willing to die for, was going away. Their sun was about to set at midday, and their whole world was going to collapse around them. In fact, the pains had already begun. The ramifications of Jesus' solemn words to the disciples there in the upper room must have staggered their minds. By John 14 they were undoubtedly bewildered, perplexed, confused, and filled with anxiety. Virtually every word Jesus says to the disciples from this point through the end of John 16 is infused with the same promise: "If I go and prepare a place for you, I will come again and will take you to myself, that where I am you may be also" (John 14:3).

Even though they were standing on the precipice of the darkest night in the history of the world, Jesus wanted them to have peace. In fact, the whole long discourse culminates at the end of John 16 with this: "I have said these things to you, that in me you may have peace. In the world you will have tribulation. But take heart; I have overcome the world" (John 16:33). He speaks of His triumph as an already-accomplished fact. Yes, He was leaving. He was, in fact, preparing to die. But this was no cause for discouragement. The conquest was already certain. Meanwhile, they must not feel abandoned; He was leaving for a good reason, and in the end all things, including this—*especially* this—would work together for their eternal good and His eternal glory.

If you have ever lost a close loved one, you know what permanent separation is like. You can only imagine the feeling of losing One who was perfect, whose fellowship was so pure, whose wisdom was so trustworthy, whose touch could heal any malady, whose strength was so reliable, whose love was so flawless. It must have been a bitter, overwhelming sense of profound loss.

On top of that, the prediction that even Peter would deny their Master must have cut like a dagger to the heart.

Chapter 14 begins where Jesus' words about Peter's failure leave off. The chapter division makes an artificial interruption at a place where there was most likely no actual pause or break in Jesus' discourse. As He predicts Peter's betrayal, Jesus anticipates and senses the crescendo of sorrow in the apostles' already breaking hearts. Now He gives them comfort upon comfort.

As we read Jesus' words in the first six verses, we can see clearly how much He cared for His disciples. He was about to be nailed to a cross, and He knew full well that He Himself would soon undergo an unimaginable deluge of woe. He would be spit on and mocked by evil men. He would bear the sins of the world. He would be cursed with the wrath of God for others' sins. He would feel as if His Father had utterly abandoned Him. Any other man in that situation would have been in such a state of uncontrollable agitation that He would never have been able to focus His attention on the needs of others—but Jesus was different.

Martin Luther called this passage "the best and most comforting sermon preached by Christ while on this earth . . . a jewel and treasure not purchasable with the world's goods."[1] These verses become the foundation for comfort, not only for those eleven disciples but also for you and me—and everyone who has ever sought refuge in Christ. If you ever get to the point in your life where you think you've run out of escapes and there aren't any more places where you can rest, you'll find a tremendously soft, downy pillow in John 14:1–6:

> "Let not your hearts be troubled. Believe in God; believe also in me. In my Father's house are many rooms. If it were not so, would I have told you that I go to prepare a place for you? And if I go and prepare a place for you, I will come again and will take you to myself, that where I am you may be also. And you know the way to where I am going."
>
> Thomas said to him, "Lord, we do not know where you are going. How can we know the way?"
>
> Jesus said to him, "I am the way, and the truth, and the life. No one comes to the Father except through me."

JESUS THE TRUE COMFORTER

Here is Jesus Christ, fully divine but nevertheless totally human, anticipating an outpouring of anguish that would literally be the most horrible experience any man would ever endure. Yet He was

---

1 Martin Luther, *Luther's Works, vol. 24: Sermons on the Gospel of St. John Chapters 14-16*, ed. Jaroslav Pelikan (St. Louis: Concordia, 1974), 7.

completely unconcerned at this point about His own experience—wholly absorbed in the needs of His eleven friends. Surely He already realized that He was about to taste the bitter cup of God's wrath in order to save sinners. He would not only die an agonizing death in a humiliating ordeal; He would also bear a world of sins and pay the awful price on behalf of others. Nevertheless His primary concern at this point lies in the sorrows and the fears of His apostles. "Having loved his own who were in the world, he loved them to the end" (John 13:1).

If there is a single, central message in John 14:1–6, it is that the basis of comfort is simple, trusting, childlike faith. If you're discontented, worried, anxious, bewildered, perplexed, confused, agitated, or otherwise in need of comfort, the answer to your dilemma is found in trusting Christ and centering all your thoughts and hopes on Him. If you really trust Him, what do you have to worry about? The reason the disciples were so stirred up is that they were focused at that moment on their own sense of loss, and they were like drowning men in a sea of sorrow. They needed a reminder to cling to their trust in Jesus; He would keep them afloat and see them through. So in these verses He reminds them of the importance of trusting Him.

In the Greek text, the command "Let not your hearts be troubled" employs a verb signifying continuous action. It could be translated, "Stop letting your hearts be troubled." The disciples were already troubled, and Jesus knew it. In fact, they were probably in a state of shock and horror. They were fully convinced that He was the promised Messiah; but the only real concept they ever had of the Messiah was as an illustrious conqueror, a kind of superhero, a sovereign ruler. Their hopes had risen even higher just a week earlier, when Jesus had come riding into Jerusalem and everyone had thrown palm branches down and worshiped Him.

But even in the midst of that, Jesus had begun to talk about His dying (John 12:23–33). How could the disciples reconcile that with their belief that He was the Messiah? And what about them? What kind of way was this to treat them? They had forsaken all and followed Him, and now He was going to forsake them. Not only that, but He was also going to leave them in the midst of enemies who hated Him and them. Nothing seemed to fit. What good was a Messiah who was going to die? Why would He get their hopes up and then leave them to be hated by all men? And where were their resources going to come from?

In addition, the Lord Himself had informed the apostles that one of their own group would be the instrument of betrayal. If Peter, who was externally the strongest of them all, would deny Him three times that very night, where did that leave the rest of them? Everything seemed to be unraveling in the worst way.

Yet even though the remaining eleven were wavering, their love for Him was undiminished. Perhaps in the midst of their fear they were hoping against hope that He would do something to reverse what must have seemed to them like an impossible situation.

Jesus, who could read their hearts like a billboard, knew exactly what they were thinking. He was touched with the feelings of their infirmities, and, in a sense, He shared their sorrows and their hurts (cf. Hebrews 4:15). They couldn't feel His pain, but He could feel theirs.

Just as Isaiah prophesied, "In all their affliction he was afflicted" (Isaiah 63:9), and, "the Lord . . . anointed [him] to bring good news to the poor . . . to bind up the brokenhearted, to proclaim liberty to the captives, and the opening of the prison to those who are bound . . . to comfort all who mourn" (61:1–2). He indeed knew "how to sustain with a word him who is weary" (50:4).

Interestingly, all the time Jesus was comforting them, He knew His disciples would scatter and forsake Him later that same night. Here was the agonizing Shepherd facing the cross, yet comforting the sheep who are about to be scattered and forsaken: "Let not your hearts be troubled."

WE CAN TRUST HIS PRESENCE

What our Lord is really saying in John 14:1 is, "You can trust My presence." He puts Himself on an equal plane with God: "Believe in God; believe also in me." In the Greek, that expression can be either imperative or indicative; both forms are the same word. In other words, He might be giving a command: "Believe in God and also in Me" (imperative); or it can be read as a statement of fact: "You believe in God, and you believe in Me" (indicative).

The statement actually makes the most sense in this context if we read the first half as indicative and the second half as imperative. To paraphrase: "You believe in God even though you can't see Him." *That's indicative.* "Now believe in Me." *That's imperative.* "Keep believing. Your faith in Me must not be diminished just because you will not see Me. I will still be present with you." He is encouraging them to keep faith, because even though He was leaving them physically, His presence would be with them spiritually. He would be returning to the Father, but He was not forsaking them. They would still have access to Him—just as they had always had access to God.

Deuteronomy 31:6 says, "Be strong and courageous. Do not fear or be in dread of them, for it is the Lord your God who goes with you. He will not leave you or forsake you." Such faith in the omnipresence of Yahweh was a basic, implicit tenet of the Jewish religion. The Jews' history was proof of His eternal care and protection. The concept of trusting in a God who could not be seen was nothing new to the disciples. Putting Himself on the same level as God, Jesus was urging them to trust Him even when He was not physically present.

People have often misinterpreted John 14:1 as a summons to saving faith. But Jesus was not saying the eleven needed to learn to believe in Him in order to be saved; they already believed in Him, and He had already assured them of their salvation (John 13:10; 15:3). John 14:1 uses a linear verb form, meaning, "Keep trusting Me, even though I will no longer be physically present with you. Keep on trusting Me just as you are trusting God."

They needed to learn to trust when they could not see—to "walk by faith, not by sight" (2 Corinthians 5:7). They all struggled with that—but none more than Thomas. You know his story: after the resurrection, he heard that Christ was alive and had appeared to others. Thomas's response was, "Unless I see in his hands the mark of the nails, and place my finger into the mark of the nails, and place my hand into his side, I will never believe" (John 20:25). Later, those were the exact conditions under which Christ met Thomas. And when Thomas finally saw for himself, he believed. The other disciples were not much different. They believed what they saw, and no more. That is the lowest level of faith.

After Jesus showed Thomas the nail prints in His hands, the Lord said, "Have you believed because you have seen me? Blessed are those who have not seen and yet have believed" (v. 29). What He was trying to get across was that His visible presence was not nearly as significant as an understanding of His spiritual presence. He is there—laboring on our behalf, interceding for us, watching over us, comforting us with His presence—even when we cannot see Him. That theme influenced everything He taught them: "Behold, I am with you always, to the end of the age" (Matthew 28:20). "I will never leave you nor forsake you" (Hebrews 13:5).

Peter clearly came to understand this truth after the ascension of Christ. Years later he wrote in 1 Peter 1:8, speaking of Christ, "Though you have not seen him, you love him. Though you do not now see him, you believe in him and rejoice with joy that is inexpressible and filled with glory." I have never seen Jesus Christ, but there is no one in existence in whom I believe more. He is alive; He is real; I know Him; I sense His presence. The Spirit of God and the Word of God continually witness to my heart about these truths.

We all live with conflict, disappointment, and pain. Most of us will experience times of deep tragedy and severe trial, but He is with us. Whatever your trouble, whatever difficulty you are in, whatever anxiety or perplexity you struggle with, just remember the Lord Himself is there. You can "[cast] all your anxieties on him, because he cares for you" (1 Peter 5:7). In a way, it is better than if He were visible, because He is not hindered by the limitations of a physical body. He can be wherever we need Him. While He was here on earth, He could be in only one place at a time. Now He is available to all believers everywhere.

WE CAN TRUST HIS PROMISES

In addition to the reassurance of His constant presence, Christ gave the disciples some wonderful promises. "In my Father's house are many rooms. If it were not so, would I have told you that I go to prepare a place for you?" (John 14:2). Most translations make this part of the statement emphatic: "If it were not so, I *would* have told you." That phrase is filled with significance. He was reassuring them that His death would not derail their hope of eternity with Him. If there had been such a change in plans, He would have said so. He was not out to trick them, and He would not allow them to be deceived.

The disciples did in fact have some presuppositions and misconceptions that needed to be corrected. They had always believed, for example, that the Messiah would be a conquering monarch, and He taught them that He must first be a suffering servant. Their hope of eternity in heaven with Him, however, was not a misconception that needed correction. In fact, He now simply wanted to reassure them that their expectation of eternity in His kingdom was not a vain hope, and His impending death and departure from them would not change that.

His leaving would be only to make heaven ready for them: "I go to prepare a place for you." Can you imagine how it must have comforted them to realize for the first time *why* He was leaving? He wasn't leaving because the messianic plan had derailed. He wasn't going to be swallowed up and taken away by death. He certainly wasn't going away just to get away from them. He was going to get things ready for them!

It is important to note that He refers to heaven as "my Father's house." Jesus' favorite name for God was "my Father." Jesus, who had dwelt forever in the bosom of the Father, came forth so that He could reveal the Father and disclose to us what the Father had been through all eternity. Now He would be glorified by death, and He was going back to full glory with the Father again in the Father's house.

In the New Testament, heaven is often called a country (emphasizing its vastness); a city (because of the large number of its inhabitants); a kingdom (because of its structure and order); and a paradise (because of its beauty). But my favorite expression for heaven is "my Father's house." I remember as a child, if I went to visit relatives, or to camp, or away from home for any reason, it was an indescribable feeling of goodness to come back to my father's house. Even after I grew up and went to college, it was wonderful to have the opportunity to go home. There I was welcome. I was accepted. I was free to be myself. I could just go right in, throw my coat off, kick off my shoes, flop into a chair, and relax. It was still as much my home as my father's.

Heaven is like that. Going home to heaven will not be like going into a giant, unfamiliar palace. We will be going home. It is our Father's house, but we will be permanent residents there. Not guests. It's home, not some place where we're uncomfortable. It's home like home has never been.

The familiar King James translation of this verse says, "In my Father's house are many mansions." That has for years given many people the wrong idea. Some of our songs about heaven reflect the misconception that it is full of big manor houses. ("I've got a mansion just over the hilltop"; "A mansion is waiting in glory"; "Have you heard of those heavenly mansions?") Some seem to think that when they arrive in heaven they'll be greeted by a heavenly real estate man, who will hand out little maps with instructions on how to get to the right hacienda. And Peter will be there with a golf cart to take you to the right lot.

But "rooms" is a more accurate rendering than "mansions." In Jesus' culture, when a son was married, he seldom left his father's house. Instead, the father would simply add another wing to the existing structure. If the father had more than one son, he would attach a new wing to the house for each son's new family. The new wings would enclose a center patio, with the different families living around it. That is the kind of arrangement John 14:2 is indicating. Jesus was not talking about tenement rooms or mansions over the hilltop but rather a single, glorious home with enough dwelling places to encompass the complete family of God. We will dwell *with* God, not down the street from Him. We will have the same patio. And there will be enough room for everyone. There will be no overcrowding, no one turned away, no "No Vacancy" signs.

Revelation 21:16 says, "The city lies foursquare, its length the same as its width. And he measured the city with his rod, 12,000 stadia. Its length and width and height are equal." Heaven, prepared uniquely for the redeemed to inhabit in glorified bodies, will be laid out like a cube. Twelve thousand "stadia" is about 15 hundred miles. That size in two dimensions is 225 million square miles. An area that size would cover almost half the continental United States. (To give a point of reference, the greater London area is 607 square miles.) If the ground floor of heaven were populated at the same ratio as London, it could hold 100 billion people with plenty of room to spare. That is far greater than the current population of our world. Twelve thousand stadia cubed is 1,728 billion cubic miles—a volume larger than any of us can conceive.

Heaven is huge, but fellowship in heaven is intimate. In Revelation 21:2–3, John reports, "And I saw the holy city, new Jerusalem, coming down out of heaven from God, prepared as a bride adorned for her husband. And I heard a loud voice from the throne saying, 'Behold, the dwelling place of God is with man. He will dwell with them, and they will be his people, and God himself will be with them as their God.'" He is there, among His people, dwelling with them in unbroken and unhindered fellowship.

John goes on. "And you know the way to where I am going" (v. 4). The Father takes care of all the hurts and the needs of the children in His house. There is no sense of need, no wanting anything, and no negative emotion.

I already feel bound to heaven. My Father is there; my Savior is there; my home is there; my name is there; my life is there; my affections are there; my heart is there; my inheritance is there; and my citizenship is there.

Heaven will be an indescribably beautiful and glorious place. Imagine what it must be like—Jesus Christ, who created the whole, magnificent universe in one week, has been laboring for two millennia preparing heaven to be the habitation of His people. Revelation 21:18–22 describes it:

The wall was built of jasper, while the city was pure gold, clear as glass. The foundations of the wall of the city were adorned with every kind of jewel. The first was jasper, the second sapphire, the third agate, the fourth emerald, the fifth onyx, the sixth carnelian, the seventh chrysolite, the eighth beryl, the ninth topaz, the tenth chrysoprase, the eleventh jacinth, the twelfth amethyst. And the twelve gates were twelve pearls, each of the gates made of a single pearl, and the street of the city was pure gold, transparent as glass. And I saw no temple in the city, for its temple is the Lord God the Almighty and the Lamb.

John goes on to write of how the glory of God will illuminate the city. Imagine the purest, brightest light flashing through the magnificent jewels in the walls. Its gates are never shut (v. 25), yet nothing defiling can enter it. What a city it will be! Transparent gold, diamond walls, and light from the Lamb's glory will form a spectacle of dazzling beauty. And the Lord Jesus is preparing it especially for His own.

"If it were not so, [I would] have told you" (John 14:2). Jesus is saying, "Trust my promises! I've always told you the truth." He continues, "And if I go and prepare a place for you, I will come again and will take you to myself, that where I am you may be also" (v. 3). What a reassurance those words must have been to the frightened disciples that dark night! As surely as Jesus was leaving, He would come again, in person, to receive them personally into the place He would prepare for them.

We can have complete confidence that He is coming back, although we do not know when. In fact, Jesus is eager to return and claim His own. In John 17:24, He prays, "Father, I desire that they also, whom you have given me, may be with me where I am, to see my glory that you have given me." Our Lord wants us with Him as much as we want to be with Him.

The truth of Jesus' second coming is on the lips of Christians all over the world. It always has been. But today there seems to be a heightened awareness, a deepening anticipation that Jesus could well come soon. In fact, He could come today. But even if He does not, we know He *will* return someday. "He cannot deny himself" (2 Timothy 2:13).

WE CAN TRUST HIS PERSON

The disciples must have been completely bewildered when Jesus, speaking of His departure, added, "And you know the way to where I am going" (John 14:4). Up to this point, they had completely resisted any idea of His leaving at all. Now they weren't certain of anything. Thomas probably spoke for the rest: "Lord, we do not know where you are going. How can we know the way?" (v. 5).

Thomas was saying, "Our knowledge stops at death. How can we go to the Father unless we die? You're going to die and go somewhere, but we don't know what's going on after death. We don't have any maps on how to get to the Father once You are gone." It was a good question.

Jesus' response is profound, and it is one of the most familiar texts in Scripture: "Jesus said to him, 'I am the way, and the truth, and the life. No one comes to the Father except through me'" (v. 6). The message in part was, "You don't need to know how to get there; I'm coming to get you." This was a reaffirmation of everything He had just promised them.

It's a beautiful promise. Have you ever been driving in an unfamiliar town and stopped to ask directions? If your experience is like mine, you've probably had someone give you a complex set of directions that you could not possibly understand. How much better it would be for the person to say, "Follow me; I'll take you there." In essence, that's what Jesus does here. He doesn't merely give the directions to the Father's house—He promises to carry us there. That's why death for the Christian is such a glorious experience. Whether we die or He literally returns to take us with Him, we know we can trust Him to take us to the Father's house.

Augustus Toplady, who wrote "Rock of Ages," died of tuberculosis in London at the age of 38. Knowing that he was dying, he shared with a friend this "Dying Avowal":

> My dear friend, those great and glorious truths, which the Lord in rich mercy has given me to believe [are not] dry doctrines or mere speculative points. No. But, being brought into practical and heart-felt experience, they are the very joy and support of my soul; and the consolations flowing from them carry me far above the things of time and sense.[2]

He added this: "Sickness is no affliction; no curse; death itself no dissolution. . . . O that I had wings like a dove, then would I flee away to the realms of bliss, and be at rest for ever! O that some angel might be commissioned, for I long to be absent from this body, and to be with my Lord for ever."[3]

About an hour before he died, Toplady seemed to awaken from a gentle slumber, and his last words were, "O what delights! Who can fathom the joys of the third heaven? [Praise God for] His abiding

---

2 Augustus Toplady, *Memoirs of the Life and Writings of the Rev. A[ugustus]. M. Toplady, B. D.,* ed. William Winters (London: F. Davis, 1872), 78.

3 Ibid., 78–79.

presence, and the shining of His love upon my soul. The sky is clear; there is no cloud: Come Lord Jesus, come quickly!"[4] And he closed his eyes.

In effect, Jesus says, "Trust Me. You don't need a map; I'm the way, the truth, and the life. I am the way to the Father. I am the truth, whether in this world or the world to come. I am the life that is eternal."

Christ is everything a man or woman needs. Everything that Adam lost—and more—is restored to us in Jesus Christ. We can trust His presence, His promises, and His person, for He is the way, the truth, and the life. I know of no greater comfort in all the world than that.

---

4 Ibid., 80.

Five

JESUS IS GOD

The strategic importance of Jesus' final hours in the upper room with His eleven remaining disciples cannot be overstated. All His instructions to them that night—His warnings, His teaching, His commandments, His promises, and His revelation—were calculated to strengthen them spiritually and brace them for the trauma they were about to undergo. It was essential that Jesus prepare them for the shock of His death. The news of His leaving was a tremendous blow to them, and their hearts were already deeply troubled. They had put all their faith in Him, and they loved Him more than life itself. Their faith might have been seriously damaged if they had seen Him die without hearing what He had to say in those few remaining hours.

The disciples had been witnesses to some amazing events in the three brief years of Jesus' ministry. He had cast out demons, healed people with every conceivable sickness, and even raised people from the dead. He had demonstrated His power over every adversary, and in every situation where it seemed He was threatened, He had come forth the victor. He had successfully countered every argument, answered every question, resisted every temptation, and confounded every enemy.

But now He was predicting His own death at the hands of wicked men.

The confused disciples did not understand how Messiah could become a victim of the people. It didn't fit their concept of what His mission would be. Not only that, but they had also become increasingly aware that Jesus was the incarnation of God. They thought of Him as invincible, omniscient, and devoid of any kind of weakness. Now they were understandably confused. Why would He die? How *could* He die? Who could defeat Him? How could anyone else ever accept Him as Messiah if He died? Did this mean that all they had lived for during the past three years was in vain? And most crucial of all, did it mean that Jesus was not who they thought He was?

Jesus, sensing the nagging questions of their troubled hearts, continued His ministry of comfort to them by reaffirming His deity:

"If you had known me, you would have known my Father also. From now on you do know him and have seen him."

Philip said to him, "Lord, show us the Father, and it is enough for us."

Jesus said to him, "Have I been with you so long, and you still do not know me, Philip? Whoever has seen me has seen the Father. How can you say, 'Show us the Father'? Do you not believe that I am in the Father and the Father is in me? The words that I say to you I do not speak on my own authority, but the Father who dwells in me does his works. Believe me that I am in the Father and the Father is in me, or else believe on account of the works themselves.

"Truly, truly, I say to you, whoever believes in me will also do the works that I do; and greater works than these will he do, because I am going to the Father. Whatever you ask in my name, this I will do, that the Father may be glorified in the Son. If you ask me anything in my name, I will do it." (John 14:7–14)

The implications of Jesus' words in those few verses are overwhelming. The fact that He claims to be God is profound enough. But then He adds a guarantee that believers in Him would have power to do even *greater* works than He had done—and He concludes by saying that if we ask anything in His name He will do it. Those words are monumental in declaring not only who Jesus is, but also what He intends to do in and for those who belong to Him.

And the passage contains three momentous revelations to His disciples and to us.

THE REVELATION OF HIS PERSON

Only a few days before, when Jesus had entered Jerusalem on the back of a donkey to shouts of "Hosanna!" there was no question in the disciples' minds about who He was. Now they weren't so sure. In their hearts they were asking questions about Him that had been answered before. Therefore, Jesus reiterated to them who He really was, by revealing His person to them in fresh and unmistakable terminology: "Whoever has seen me has seen the Father" (v. 9). "I am in the Father and the Father is in me" (v. 10).

What did He reveal to them about Himself? One thing: *He is God.* They had heard His claims of deity before, and they had witnessed the proof of it in His works. He had just said that He was the way to God, the truth about God, and the very life of God (v. 6). He goes a step further in verses 7–10 and says in unequivocal terms that He *is* God. His words must have been staggering, because the claim is so tremendous.

Yet it cannot be dismissed. No fair-minded person can ignore or gloss over Jesus' claim to be God. The single, central, most important issue of all about Jesus is the question of His deity. Everyone who studies the life of Jesus must confront the issue, because of what the New Testament teaches. The most common view is that Jesus' claim to be God was false, but He was a good teacher anyway and worth listening to. Others judge more harshly, concluding that Jesus was a madman with delusions of grandeur. Still others believe He was a deliberate fraud.

Regarding these opinions, C. S. Lewis famously observed that "the one thing we must not say about Jesus is that He is a great moral teacher but not God. Good teachers don't claim to be God. Either He was indeed God in the flesh, or else He was a madman or a fraud." Lewis further noted:

> A man who was merely a man and said the sort of things Jesus said would not be a great moral teacher. He would either be a lunatic—on a level with the man who says he is a poached egg—or else he would be the Devil of Hell. You must make your choice. Either this man was, and is, the Son of God: or else a madman or something worse.[1]

Sabellius, a third-century heretic and the forerunner of the Unitarian sect, taught that Jesus was only a radiation, a manifestation of God. But He is *not* merely a manifestation of God; He is God manifest.

---

1 C. S. Lewis, *Mere Christianity* (New York: Macmillan, 1960), 41.

There is a significant difference. Jesus is uniquely one with, but distinct from, the Father—God in human flesh.

In John 14:7–10 Jesus makes the very simple, undisguised claim that He is no less than God Himself. He had told the apostles many times in the past that He had come from the Father. His comment in verse 4 implies that they should have understood: *"You know the way to where I am going."* They should have at least known that He was going to be with the Father. But Jesus' words left them scratching their heads, and Thomas asked for an explanation. Jesus' answer was simply, "I am the way, and the truth, and the life. No one comes to the Father except through me" (v. 6).

That was a straightforward claim of divine authority. In other words, "I am truth incarnate, and if you know Me, you know the way to get where I'm going. I'm going to the Father; and I'll take you." He reinforced that claim with a mild rebuke for their unbelief and a reassurance that they were as secure in their relationship with the Father as they were in their relationship with the Son: "If you had known me, you would have known my Father also. From now on you do know him and have seen him" (v. 7).

In a sense, the disciples did not even know Jesus as they should have. If they had really known Him, they wouldn't have been worried about where the Father was.

Obviously, they did have a basic knowledge of who Jesus was. They had declared that He was Messiah, the anointed one of God. Peter had even made the statement that He was the Son of the living God (Matthew 16:16). They were very close to grasping fully the truth of His deity and beginning to understand the meaning of it. Nevertheless, they were still confused, so Jesus stated it in the clearest possible language, in terms they could not possibly miss: "If you had known me, you would have known my Father also. From now on you do know him and have seen him. . . . Whoever has seen me has seen the Father. . . . I am in the Father and the Father is in me" (vv. 7–10).

Jesus was telling His disciples, "If you really knew Me in depth, you would know the Father also. Your confusion about the Father means that there must be some gaps in your knowledge of Me." If they had really seen Jesus fully as God, they would not have had fears, doubts, and questions about who the Father was and how to get to Him. Months before this, when some unbelieving Pharisees demanded to see the Father, Jesus answered them: "You know neither me nor my Father. If you knew me, you would know my Father also" (John 8:19). Here Jesus makes essentially the same point to the eleven disciples in the upper room, but the rebuke He gives them is much milder.

Remember, Jesus' words were meant to comfort them. They knew He loved them. He wanted them to know that God the Father cared for them in the same way, because He and the Father are One. To have a relationship with One is to have a relationship with the other. That is an important, eternal principle. "Whoever does not honor the Son does not honor the Father who sent him" (John 5:23). If you reject the Son, you have rejected the Father; and if you receive the Son, you have received the Father. The apostle John grasped this in its fullness, and it became a theme of his ministry. Years later he would write, "No one who denies the Son has the Father. Whoever confesses the Son has the Father also" (1 John 2:23).

But it appears that none of the disciples immediately understood the full import of what Jesus was telling them. His words, "From now on you do know him and have seen him" (v. 7), are more a prediction than a proclamation. It's an echo of John 13:7: "What I am doing you do not understand now, but afterward you will understand." The expression "from now on" in John 14:7 does not mean "from this precise moment on," because Jesus knew they did not yet grasp what He was saying. (In fact, verse 8 reveals Philip still didn't fully understand who Jesus was.)

Similarly, "you do know him and have seen him" does not mean the disciples now completely understood everything about Trinitarian orthodoxy. Jesus was using the idiom of His day. He spoke in the present tense to signify the ultimate certainty of what He was saying. The message to the disciples is, "Starting now, you are going to begin to understand." Through the events that were about to take place—the death of Jesus Christ, His resurrection, His ascension, and the coming of the Holy Spirit—they would come to understand more fully about Jesus' person and His relationship to the Father.

And that is exactly what happened. Thomas, for example, had doubted the resurrection even after hearing eyewitness testimony. But when he saw Christ, it all fell into place—finally—and he understood who Jesus was. He looked at the risen Lord and Savior and said, "My Lord and my God!" (John 20:28).

Philip's request in John 14:8, "Lord, show us the Father, and it is enough for us" proved that the disciples, during their time in the upper room, did not see the full truth of who Jesus is. It was a shallow, faithless, ignorant thing to say, and it revealed that Philip's knowledge of God was incomplete. So he did what people have done throughout history: he asked to see.

Philip wanted to walk by sight rather than by faith. It wasn't enough for him to believe; he wanted to see something. It could be that he remembered the account of Exodus 33, when Moses was tucked behind a rock and saw the afterglow of God's glory pass by. Or maybe he recalled the words of Isaiah 40:5: "The glory of the Lord shall be revealed, and all flesh shall see it together, for the mouth of the Lord has spoken."

Perhaps. But I don't think Philip was an Old Testament scholar at all. He was a disciple with weak and fragile faith who wanted sight to substitute for faith. We can understand his feelings. It would be a lot easier to tolerate Jesus' departure if the disciples could first have a glimpse of the Father, just to make certain Jesus really knew where He was going. It would be much easier to cling to Jesus' promise that He would come again to get them if God would personally confirm it. If Jesus could do that, there would be no doubt about the validity of His claims. God Himself would be a guarantee that Jesus' pledge was secure.

Philip's question was an eery echo of what those unbelieving Pharisees in John 8 had demanded. They said, "Where is your Father?" (John 8:19). Philip said, "Show us the Father, and it is enough for us." The question revealed a gross deficiency in Philip's faith, and Jesus gave him essentially the same answer He had given the unbelieving Jews: "Have I been with you so long, and you still do not know me, Philip? Whoever has seen me has seen the Father. How can you say, 'Show us the Father'?" (14:9). That was, of course, a rebuke to Philip, but I believe there was also pathos in the voice of Jesus. Can you imagine the heartbreak of Jesus after He had poured His life into these twelve men for three years, to know that one of them was a traitor, one of them a profane denier, and the other ten men of little faith? It was the night before His death, and they still didn't really know who He was.

Imagine Philip, standing there staring Christ in the face and asking Him to show him God. Jesus' answer to him was, "Open your eyes. You've been looking at me for three years." Those who had seen Jesus had seen the visible manifestation of God. The writer of Hebrews says. "[Jesus Christ] is the radiance of the glory of God and the exact imprint of his nature" (Hebrews 1:3). The apostle Paul declares, "He is the image of the invisible God" (Colossians 1:15), and "in him the whole fullness of deity dwells bodily" (2:9). Jesus is God.

It is easy to see how unbelievers might say what Philip did. But for him to ask to see the Father as proof of Jesus' claims was a clumsy, inexcusable, personal affront to Jesus. Philip and the other disciples had seen Jesus' works and heard His words for three years. Jesus had never given them any reason to doubt Him.

Anyone who has ever discipled a newer believer must know something of Jesus' frustration in the face of Philip's unbelief. But Jesus was not discouraged; He had gone as far as He could with the disciples, and now He was ready to turn them over to the Holy Spirit. That is a good principle to apply in discipleship.

Jesus' answer might not have seemed very satisfying to Philip, but it was exactly what Philip needed. Jesus didn't do any miracles for him or give him any great display of power; He simply commanded him to believe: "Do you not believe that I am in the Father and the Father is in me? The words that I say to you I do not speak on my own authority, but the Father who dwells in me does his works. Believe me that I am in the Father and the Father is in me, or else believe on account of the works themselves" (John 14:10–11). Philip asked for sight; Jesus told him to seek faith instead.

Christianity is all about believing. If you think the height of spirituality is to see miracles, hear the voice of God booming out of the ceiling, or experience various supernatural phenomena, you don't have a clue regarding what believing God is really all about. Satan can duplicate all those things in counterfeit. If you want manifestations or supernatural power, you can get them at a séance.

Christianity is walking by faith, not sight. I have never seen Jesus, never had a vision, never seen angelic hosts, never heard heavenly voices, and never been carried into the third heaven. Yet my spiritual eyes can see things that my physical eyes could never even conceive of. I don't want visions, miracles, and strange phenomena. I want one thing—I want what the disciples prayed for in Luke 17:5: "Increase our faith!"

Faith is not as one little boy described it: "Believing in something you know ain't so." In fact, faith is just the opposite—believing in something you know *is* so. Genuine faith has an essential basis in fact.

The disciples certainly had an objective, factual basis for their faith. And Jesus reemphasized that to Philip: "The words that I say to you I do not speak on my own authority, but the Father who dwells in me does his works. Believe me that I am in the Father and the Father is in me, or else believe on account of the works themselves" (John 14:10–11). If Philip and the others had truly been listening for the past three years, if they had really paid attention to the works Jesus did, they would not have doubted now.

There is always a danger of doubting in the darkness things that we have seen clearly in the light. That's what the disciples were doing. During the three years of Jesus' earthly ministry they had repeatedly heard and seen proof that He was God incarnate. Now their faith was wavering, in spite of the solid, factual foundation upon which it was built. They had heard all His claims, all His teachings, all His insights probing into hidden truths, all His words revealing a supernatural knowledge of the human heart. He had already answered all their deepest, most heartfelt questions—even the ones not articulated out loud. And if His words were not sufficient proof, they had the testimony of His works, His miracles, and His sinless life.

Philip's request to see God, then, was a gross and inappropriate display of unbelief. He didn't need to see anything; Jesus had proved His deity. What more could He show the disciples? He was God incarnate. In addition to observing His words and works, they had experienced

His love for them. Therefore, at this point, how could one of them possibly ask to see God?

And so He reaffirmed to the eleven the tremendous revelation that He is God. If they could grasp that truth, they could rest easy, knowing they were secure.

THE REVELATION OF HIS POWER

Next, He revealed to them the incredible resource of power they had available through Him. "Truly, truly, I say to you, whoever believes in me will also do the works that I do; and greater works than these will he do, because I am going to the Father" (John 14:12). Christians over the centuries have wondered at the richness of such a promise. What does it mean? How could anyone do greater works than Jesus had done? He had healed people blind from birth, cast out the most powerful demons, and even raised Lazarus from the dead after four days in the grave. What could possibly be greater than those miracles?

The key to understanding this promise is in the last phrase of verse 12: "because I am going to the Father." When Jesus went to the Father, He sent the Holy Spirit. The Spirit's power completely transformed the disciples from a group of fearful, timid individuals into a cohesive force that reached the world with the gospel. The impact of their preaching exceeded even the impact of Jesus' public teaching ministry during His lifetime. Jesus never preached outside a 175-mile radius extending from His birthplace. Within His lifetime, Europe never received word of the gospel. But under the ministry of the disciples the good news began to spread, and it's still spreading today. Their works were greater than His, not in power, but in scope. Through the indwelling Holy Spirit, each one of those disciples had access to power in dimensions they did not previously have, even with the physical presence of Christ.

The disciples undoubtedly thought that without Christ they would be reduced to nothing. He was the source of their strength; how could they have power without Him? His promise was meant to ease those fears. If they felt secure in His presence, they would be even more secure, more powerful, able to do more, if He returned to the Father and sent the Holy Spirit.

The disciples had power to work great miracles. Acts 5:12–15 says that "many signs and wonders were regularly done among the people by the hands of the apostles. And they were all together in Solomon's Portico. None of the rest dared join them, but the people held them in high esteem. And more than ever believers were added to the Lord, multitudes of both men and women, so that they even carried out the sick into the streets and laid them on cots and mats, that as Peter came by at least his shadow might fall on some of them." Acts 2:40–41 records that Peter preached and three thousand people were saved. That never happened during the ministry of Jesus. He never saw widespread revival. The gospel never went to the Gentiles while He was on earth. But through the works of His apostles after He departed, conversions took place everywhere.

And after all, the greatest miracle God can perform is salvation. Every time we introduce someone to faith in Jesus Christ, we are observers of the new birth; we are supporting the most important spiritual work in the world. How exciting it is to be involved in what God is doing spiritually and to do things greater than even Jesus saw in His day.

THE REVELATION OF HIS PROMISE

Finally, Jesus gave the apostles a promise meant to ease the grief they felt at His leaving: "Whatever you ask in my name, this I will do, that the Father may be glorified in the Son. If you ask me anything in my name, I will do it" (John 14:13–14).

Jesus had fed them. He had helped them catch their fish. On one occasion He had even provided Peter's tax money out of the mouth of a fish. He had supplied all their needs. But now He was leaving, and they must have wondered, *How are we going to get a job? How are we going to fit back into society? What will we do without Him?*

Jesus' disciples had left everything and were completely without resources. Without their Master, they would be all alone in a hostile world. Yet, He assured them, they did not need to worry about any of their needs. The gap between Him and them would be closed instantly whenever they prayed. Even though He would be absent, they would have access to all His supplies.

That is not carte blanche for every whim of the flesh. There's a qualifying statement repeated twice. He doesn't say, "I'll give you *absolutely anything* you ask for," but rather, "I'll do what you ask *in My name.*" That does not mean we can simply tack the words "in-Jesus'-name-amen" on the end of our prayers and expect the answers we want every time. Neither is it a special formula or abracadabra that will magically guarantee the granting of our every wish.

The name of Jesus stands for all that He is. Throughout Scripture, God's names are the same as His attributes. When Isaiah prophesied that Messiah would be called "Wonderful Counselor, Mighty God, Everlasting Father, Prince of Peace" (9:6), he was not listing actual names, but rather giving an overview of Messiah's character. "I am who I am," the name revealed to Moses in Exodus 3:14, is as much an affirmation of God's eternal nature as it is a name by which He is to be called.

Therefore, praying in the name of Jesus is more than merely mentioning His name at the end of our prayers. If we are truly praying in Jesus' name, we will pray only for that which is consistent with His perfect character, and for that which will bring glory to Him. It implies an acknowledgment of all that He has done and a submission to His will.

What praying in Jesus' name really means is that we should pray as if our Lord Himself were doing the asking. We approach the throne of the Father in full identification with the Son, seeking only what He would seek. When we pray with that perspective, we begin to pray for the things that really matter, and we eliminate selfish requests. When we pray that way, His promise is, "I will do it" (John 14:14). That is a guarantee that, within His will, we cannot lack anything. His concern for His own transcends all circumstances, so that "neither death nor life, nor angels nor rulers, nor things present nor things to come, nor powers, nor height nor depth, nor anything else in all creation, will be able to separate us from the love of God in Christ Jesus our Lord" (Romans 8:38–39).

John 14:13–14 is the heart of Jesus' message of comfort to His terrified disciples, and it must have been tremendously reassuring to hear those words and ponder them. In the midst of the collapse of their dreams and hopes, He gave them Himself as the Rock to which they could cling and under which they could seek shelter.

Jesus Christ cares no less for those who are His disciples today. His promises are still valid; His power has not diminished; and His person is unchanging. We do not have the benefit of His physical presence, but we have His Holy Spirit. And although we cannot see Jesus, we can sense His love for us as the Spirit sheds it abroad in our hearts. In many ways, we know Him better than if we knew Him from His physical presence alone. As the apostle Peter encourages us, "Though you have not seen him, you love him. Though you do not now see him, you believe in him and rejoice with joy that is inexpressible and filled with glory, obtaining the outcome of your faith, the salvation of your souls" (1 Peter 1:8–9).

What a thrill it is to experience His love in this way, and what a comfort to know that He is God, and He cares for us.

---×◇×---

Six

THE COMING
OF THE COMFORTER

You cannot study the New Testament long without realizing there is a dichotomy between what we as Christians are responsible to do versus what God has already done on our behalf. To understand the distinction is to get a grip on the basics of our faith.

On the one hand, we are told repeatedly in Scripture how we are to live, act, think, and speak. We are enjoined to be this or to refrain from that. We are informed about what we are to do, at what point we are to commit ourselves, and for what tasks we are to separate ourselves. All of that is essential to our Christian faith.

On the other hand, much of the New Testament emphasizes what Christ has already done for us. We are told that we are called, justified, sanctified, and kept in the faith through no effort of our own. We learn that Christ and the Holy Spirit are continually interceding on our behalf. And we discover that we are the recipients of an inheritance that cannot be measured in human terms.

Most of Jesus' final discourse to His disciples consists of *promises,* not *commandments.* He spent the evening telling them what He would do for them rather than listing rules and instructions for them to obey. That, by the way, reflects the very essence of gospel truth. In contrast to the law, which issues orders and threatens condemnation, the gist of the gospel is good news about what God has done to save sinners.

John 14:15–26 is the heart of Jesus' message of comfort to the disciples. This section starts with a definitive statement about the importance of obeying Jesus' commands, but our Lord quickly shifts into promise mode:

> "If you love me, you will keep my commandments. And I will ask the Father, and he will give you another Helper, to be with you forever, even the Spirit of truth, whom the world cannot receive, because it neither sees him nor knows him. You know him, for he dwells with you and will be in you.
>
> "I will not leave you as orphans; I will come to you. Yet a little while and the world will see me no more, but you will see me. Because I live, you also will live. In that day you will know that I am in my Father, and you in me, and I in you. Whoever has my commandments and keeps them, he it is who loves me. And he who loves me will be loved by my Father, and I will love him and manifest myself to him."
>
> Judas (not Iscariot) said to him, "Lord, how is it that you will manifest yourself to us, and not to the world?"
>
> Jesus answered him, "If anyone loves me, he will keep my word, and my Father will love him, and we will come to him and make our home with him. Whoever does not love me does not keep my words. And the word that you hear is not mine but the Father's who sent me.
>
> "These things I have spoken to you while I am still with you. But the Helper, the Holy Spirit, whom the Father will

send in my name, he will teach you all things and bring to your remembrance all that I have said to you."

The promises Jesus makes here are staggering. The centerpiece of the whole section is the greatest promise of all: After His departure, the Holy Spirit would come in His place. A series of related promises go with that one.

To whom does Jesus make them? Jesus is speaking to His eleven disciples, of course, but the scope of His promises is broader than that. Verse 15 says, "If you love me, you will keep my commandments." That, of course, applies to all of us, and since all the subsequent promises are attached to it, the implied corollary is that the promises likewise must also have some application to everyone who loves Jesus Christ (see 14:21–24). In other words, they have principles and applications that are relevant to all true believers in Christ, those whose love for Him is demonstrated in their obedience.

We cannot miss the significance of Jesus' clear statement here that the proof of genuine love for Him is obedience to His commandments. The New Testament consistently teaches that love for Christ and submission to Him are necessary expressions of authentic belief. The apostle Paul refers to Christians as "all who love our Lord Jesus Christ with love incorruptible" (Ephesians 6:24). Elsewhere he says, "If anyone has no love for the Lord, let him be accursed" (1 Corinthians 16:22). Furthermore, "Faith apart from works is useless" (James 2:20). Many unbelievers "profess to know God, but they deny him by their works" (Titus 1:16). Christian obedience is defined as "faith working through love" (Galatians 5:6).

Jesus Himself frequently stressed the necessity of obedience: "Not everyone who says to me, 'Lord, Lord,' will enter the kingdom of heaven, but the one who does the will of my Father who is in heaven"

(Matthew 7:21). "Blessed . . . are those who hear the word of God and keep it!" (Luke 11:28). He repeats the point a second, third, and fourth time in our passage: "Whoever has my commandments and keeps them, he it is who loves me" (John 14:21). "If anyone loves me, he will keep my word. . . . Whoever does not love me does not keep my words" (vv. 23–24).

Love for Christ is not sentimentalism or a sickly, pseudospiritual feeling. It does not result in mere lip service, either. Real love for Him is demonstrated by an active, eager, joyful, responsive obedience to His commandments. What you say about your love for Him is relatively unimportant—what counts is that you show your love for Him by how you live your life. Discipleship is not singing songs and saying nice things. True discipleship is obedience, motivated by love.

To those who are bound to Him by their love, the Lord extends a number of promises. These promises are for all disciples from all time periods since Christ ascended. They are not rewards in return for our faithfulness; they are gracious gifts from God to aid and encourage us in obedience. They are benefits God has provided us without any effort on our part. All of them are tied to the coming of the Holy Spirit, the Comforter, Teacher, and Helper who would minister to the disciples when Jesus left. Together, these promises constitute the legacy our Lord bequeaths to His disciples—starting with the eleven, but extending to everyone who loves Christ.

THE INDWELLING SPIRIT

The promise of the Holy Spirit is the culmination of all that Jesus had to say to comfort His eleven troubled disciples. In that hour of turmoil, they feared being left alone. Jesus assured them that they would not be left to fend for themselves, but they would have a supernatural

Helper. The Greek word for "Helper" is *parakletos,* which literally means "one who is called *[kaleo]* alongside *[para].*" (We sometimes use the term *Paraclete,* even in English, to signify the Holy Spirit.) The King James Version translates the expression as "Comforter," which is another one of its meanings. Jesus is saying, "I am going to send a Helper, a Comforter—one to stand alongside you."

The Greek word translated "another" is crucial to an understanding of Jesus' full meaning. The Greek language, with all its complexities, is much more precise than English. Ancient Koine Greek had two words that meant "another." One was *heteros,* which means "a different kind," as in, "This wrench doesn't fit; bring me another one." *Allos* also means "another," but it means "another of the same kind," as in "I enjoyed that sandwich; I think I'll have another."

Allos is the word Jesus used to describe the Holy Spirit: "another *[allos]* helper." He is, in effect, saying, "I am sending you One of exactly the same essence as Me." The disciples would have known His meaning immediately. He was not sending just any old helper, but One exactly like Himself, with the same compassion, the same attributes of deity, and the same love for them.

Jesus had been their *Paraclete* for three years. He had helped them, comforted them, and walked alongside them. Now they would have another Helper—One exactly like Jesus—to minister to them as He had.

The Holy Spirit is not a mystical power or ethereal force; He is a person as much as Jesus is a person. He is not a floating fog or some kind of ghostlike emanation. It is unfortunate that the King James translators used the term "Ghost" instead of "Spirit" to translate the Greek *pneuma.* For generations people have had the erroneous idea that the Holy Spirit is something like the comic-book character Casper the Friendly Ghost. He is, however, not a ghost, but a person.

All believers have two Paracletes—the Spirit of God within us, and

Christ at the right hand of the Father in heaven. First John 2:1 says, "My little children, I am writing these things to you so that you may not sin. But if anyone does sin, we have an advocate with the Father, Jesus Christ the righteous." The word translated "advocate" in that verse is *parakletos.*

You can imagine the disciples must have been greatly encouraged and comforted to hear Jesus say He would send another helper like Him to minister to them in His place after He ascended. As One who possesses exactly the same divine essence as Christ, the Holy Spirit would be a perfect substitute for Jesus' familiar presence.

But our Lord's promise extended beyond that. The final phrase in John 14:16 beautifully extends the promise of comfort over the horizon of time and into eternity: "He will give you another Helper, to be with you forever." Not only would the Holy Spirit come to dwell with them—He would never leave. Once the Spirit of God resides within a person, He is there forever.

In Luke 11:13, Jesus told His disciples the Father would give them the Holy Spirit if they asked. Yet here, before they can even ask, He asks on their behalf. That is a good picture of how our prayers operate. The Lord knows what we have need of before we even ask. Speaking prophetically in Isaiah 65:24, the Lord says, "Before they call I will answer; while they are yet speaking I will hear." I'm sure that often, before we even get our prayers organized, Christ has already presented those needs to the Father. That is part of His ministry of advocacy and intercession.

SPIRITUAL PERCEPTION

Notice that the Spirit is called "the Spirit of truth" (John 14:17). He is both the living essence of truth (because He is God) and the One who guides us into all truth. In fact, unbelievers cannot recognize the Spirit or His work, and that is as Jesus said it would be: "The Spirit of truth, whom the world cannot receive, because it neither sees him nor knows him" (John 14:17). The world didn't recognize the first Comforter, Jesus. Much less could those who are spiritually blind recognize the second One, whose character and essence are exactly like the first, but He cannot be seen with eyes of flesh.

Unregenerate people have no facility for spiritual perception. They have no way to see the working of the power of the Holy Spirit. When the academic minds of Jesus' day came to their conclusion about who He was, their very astute, reasoned, theological pronouncement was that He was from the Devil (Matthew 12:24)—and that came after a long time of studying His ministry. That shows graphically the spiritual capacity of the unregenerate. Given all the facts, unbelievers will invariably conclude the wrong thing.

In 1 Corinthians 2:12–14, the apostle Paul writes,

Now we have received not the spirit of the world, but the Spirit who is from God, that we might understand the things freely given us by God.

And we impart this in words not taught by human wisdom but taught by the Spirit, interpreting spiritual truths to those who are spiritual. The natural person does not accept the things of the Spirit of God, for they are folly to him, and he is not able to understand them because they are spiritually discerned.

In other words, the only way a person can understand the things of God is to have the Spirit of God. The natural man cannot understand the Holy Spirit's work. "For the mind that is set on the flesh is hostile to God, for it does not submit to God's law; indeed, it cannot. Those who are in the flesh cannot please God" (Romans 8:7–8).

That is why Jesus indicted the Jewish leaders for clinging to their natural understanding of spiritual matters:

> You are of your father the devil, and your will is to do your father's desires. He was a murderer from the beginning, and has nothing to do with the truth, because there is no truth in him. When he lies, he speaks out of his own character, for he is a liar and the father of lies. But because I tell the truth, you do not believe me. . . . Why do you not believe me? Whoever is of God hears the words of God. The reason why you do not hear them is that you are not of God. (John 8:44–45, 47)

As unregenerate men, they had no capacity to comprehend the truth of God.

So Jesus told His disciples that when the Holy Spirit came, the people of the world would not get the message. He was right, of course. In Acts 2, when the Holy Spirit descended on the day of Pentecost, the unbelievers who witnessed the manifestation thought the disciples were drunk. The Holy Spirit was just as foreign to the stubborn, rejecting world as Jesus had been.

When I first studied John 14, I was puzzled about why in that context Jesus told the disciples the world would not respond to the Holy Spirit. Then it became clear that with all the promises Jesus was giving them, they might have succumbed to overconfidence. He had told them they would do greater things than even He had done (v. 12), and He had promised to answer every prayer they asked (v. 14). If the Lord had not given the disciples a clear and complete perspective beforehand, they might have been totally deflated when they first encountered rejection. Jesus was simply trying to give them a tempered, balanced response.

The Eternal Union with God

At the end of John 14:17, our Lord reaffirms a classic biblical truth: "You know him, for he dwells with you and will be in you." They knew of the ministry of God's Spirit from the Old Testament. In the Old Testament economy the Spirit of God sometimes came upon specially anointed people to empower them for some singular work, and after the task was accomplished, He would usually depart. The Holy Spirit came on Saul, Azariah, and Isaiah, for example. In the case of Samson, Scripture repeatedly says, "The Spirit of the Lord *rushed* upon him"— enabling him to exhibit superhuman strength (Judges 14:6, 19; 15:14, emphasis added). But when Samson broke a lifelong vow by allowing his hair to be cut, Scripture says, "the Lord . . . left him"—meaning the Spirit withdrew His spiritual anointing, His supernatural strength, and His presence from Samson (Judges 16:20).

That's emblematic of the Spirit's ministry in the Old Testament economy. He often empowered people for special service, revealed truth to the prophets, and was active in many ways from creation (Genesis 1:2) to the baptism of Christ—when the Spirit descended on Jesus like a dove (Luke 3:22). So the disciples were not ignorant of the ministry of the Spirit. But there's no suggestion in Scripture that the Holy Spirit permanently indwelt anyone. He was constantly present and active among the people of God, but not in permanent spiritual union with each believer. That aspect of His ministry to Christians seems to be something new and unique in the New Testament era.

Notice Jesus' words: "he dwells *with* you and will be *in* you" (v. 17, emphasis added). The Holy Spirit would no longer merely be present in their midst; He would now be spiritually in union with them—and the Greek verb tense indicates that this would be a permanent, uninterrupted abiding within.

107

That kind of relationship is never mentioned in the Old Testament, except in prophecies about the New Covenant. It is a fulfillment of the promise given in Ezekiel 37:14: "And I will put my Spirit within you, and you shall live." That promise is one of the key features that distinguishes between the Old and New Covenants.

Although the Spirit's role changed somewhat from Old to New Covenant, His essential person and character remain the same. He is the same Spirit. The difference is that in the New Testament the mystery regarding who He is and how He works has been removed. And each believer is now intimately in union with Him, permanently.[1]

What a privilege it is in the grace of God that He would plant His very essence in us! We have a supernatural Helper, not just "with" us, but *within* us. Every moment of our existence throughout all eternity, we have the abiding presence of the Holy Spirit within (cf. John 7:37–39; Acts 1:8; 2:1–4; 19:1–7; 1 Corinthians 12:11–13).

THE PRESENCE OF CHRIST

Our Lord expands the promise in John 14:18–19: "I will not leave you as orphans; I will come to you. Yet a little while and the world will see me no more, but you will see me." Their Master and mentor was dying. He would literally be dead before another full day had passed, and He knew it. He wanted to reassure the disciples that they could nevertheless count on His presence after that.

There are at least two elements involved in this promise. For one thing, Christ was guaranteeing His followers that He would rise from the dead. His dying on the cross would not be the end of His

---

1 For a complete discussion of the Spirit's person and work in the Old Testament, see chapter 2, "The Spirit in the Old Testament," in John MacArthur, *The Silent Shepherd* (Wheaton, IL: Victor, 1996), 23–40.

existence. But beyond that, He promised, "I will come to you." Some say that this is a promise of the return of Christ for His people. But if this verse referred to that, it would say, "I will come *for* you." Others say it is only a promise that the disciples would see Him after the resurrection. I don't think that's the best interpretation either, because He was on earth only forty days after He arose. Such a short time frame seems a comparatively small measure of comfort.

I believe Jesus is here speaking of His spiritual presence in every believer through the agency of the Holy Spirit. He is saying, "When the Spirit of God comes to reside in you, I will be there as well." In Matthew 28:20, He promises, "behold, I am with you always, to the end of the age."

This is the mystery of the Trinity: the Holy Spirit abides in us (John 14:17). Christ indwells us (Colossians 1:27). And God is in us (1 John 4:12). We are fully united spiritually with each member of the Godhead, and that is the source of eternal life. Jesus goes on to say, "Because I live, you also will live" (John 14:19).

How is it that a person can sense the presence of God within him? How can he know the Spirit of God is there? How can he know that the Son of God lives within? He must be spiritually alive to have spiritual perception. The spiritually dead individual understands nothing about God; he cannot respond to God.

But the person who is spiritually alive lives in another dimension. He is alive to the spiritual realm. And the source and basis of his life is the resurrection of Jesus Christ: "Because I live, you also will live." When Scripture speaks of "eternal life," it isn't merely talking about the quantity or duration of the redeemed life. It's a reference to the kind of life that makes a person sensitive and aware of that realm of glory where God Himself abides. Here is the essence of spiritual life: to be alive spiritually, walking with God, sensing the Holy Spirit, communing with Christ, and moving and participating in the spiritual realm. The world cannot know anything about that.

FULL UNDERSTANDING

Jesus Himself describes for us what it means to be *indwelt* by the Holy Spirit, Christ, and the Father. It is, as we have been saying, a *spiritual union* with each member of the Trinity. Jesus compares it with His relationship to the Father: "In that day you will know that I am in my Father, and you in me, and I in you" (John 14:20). We are spiritually one with God and Christ—living temples for the Holy Spirit. That's why sin is so out of place in the believer's life: "Do you not know that your body is a temple of the Holy Spirit within you, whom you have from God? You are not your own, for you were bought with a price. So glorify God in your body" (1 Corinthians 6:19–20).

It is confusing to try to understand how we can be at the same time in Christ and He in us. At first glance that doesn't seem logical. Think of it like an infusion of fluids. Put chocolate syrup in a glass of milk, and you have milk in your chocolate and chocolate in your milk. It is a complete and perfect union of two distinct substances. We are so closely united spiritually with our Lord that He is in us and we in Him.

That night in the upper room, the disciples still seemed mostly mystified about the relation of the Son to the Father. Union with deity was such a foreign concept to them that their minds could not conceive of it. So Jesus told them, "In that day you will know that I am in my Father, and you in me, and I in you." It seems clear that He was referring to the day of Pentecost, in which the Holy Spirit descended on them permanently. Before the Spirit came to dwell within them and teach them the truth, they had no way of understanding the relationship of Christ with His Father, nothing to compare such a relationship with, and no idea how it corresponded to their relationship with the Godhead.

But when they received the Holy Spirit in Acts 2, they began to understand. Peter is probably the best evidence of that. Bumbling, faltering Peter, who rarely seemed to understand anything clearly, stood up on the very day that the Spirit of God came to dwell within him and preached one of the most powerful sermons ever to come from a redeemed sinner's lips. He clearly delineated exactly who Jesus Christ is, why He rose from the grave, what the will of the Father is, and what it all meant in reference to Israel and the Old Testament Scriptures.

Peter had not secretly acquired a seminary education or read all the good theology books—those things weren't even available. The Spirit of God had supernaturally untangled Peter's previous confusion, and everything suddenly fell into place for him.

THE MANIFESTATION OF THE FATHER

In a beautiful summary, crushing the full bloom of redemption into one little wisp of fragrance, Jesus reviews how to identify the person who has come into that supernatural union with Him: "Whoever has my commandments and keeps them, he it is who loves me. And he who loves me will be loved by my Father, and I will love him and manifest myself to him" (John 14:21). He has come full circle to the point at which He began in verse 15.

The Father wants to glorify the Son, and He continually does so. He does so through the Spirit, who pours the love of God into His people's hearts (Romans 5:5). The best way to discern whom God has set His redemptive love on is by discerning who truly loves the Son. Those who love Christ are loved by the Father. That is not difficult to understand from a human perspective. I want people to like my children. How much more must that be true with God, whose love is perfect?

But understand this: God's love for His people is not a reward bestowed on them because they loved Christ. The opposite is true. "We love because he first loved us" (1 John 4:19).

Those who love Christ are loved by Him as well, because Jesus loves what His Father loves. And He promises to manifest Himself to them. Occasionally you will hear some well-meaning Christian suggest that Christianity is not a religion but a relationship. In reality, being a devoted disciple of Christ entails *both* "religion that is pure and undefiled before God" (James 1:27) *and* an intimate relationship with Christ. Still, the point Jesus is making here is, I believe, the truth people seem to be fumbling to express when they disparage religion in favor of the language of personal relationships. True obedience to Christ stems from a loving relationship with Him (v. 15). The obedience Jesus calls for is not a mechanical religious ritual that simply goes through the motions—keeping the exterior of the cup clean, going to church, sleepwalking through a liturgy, reciting the responsive readings by rote, and taking care to be seen by others in the process. Real obedience to Christ flows from an honest, deep, heartfelt, committed love that obeys. That is someone whom Christ loves and to whom He has manifested Himself as Savior.

I am sure all the disciples were dumbfounded at this point in Jesus' discourse. Judas—not Iscariot, but the son of James (Luke 6:16; Acts 1:13), who, by the way, is also called Lebbaeus and Thaddaeus—spoke out: "Lord, how is it that you will manifest yourself to us, and not to the world?" (John 14:22). He thought Jesus meant that He would physically manifest Himself and the Father, perhaps in some kind of cosmic, apocalyptic display. How could that not be seen by the whole world? The disciples no doubt reasoned that if they could see Jesus, everyone else should be able to see Him as well. Furthermore, Christ was to be the Savior of the world. How could He not manifest Himself to the world?

"Jesus answered him, 'If anyone loves me, he will keep my word, and my Father will love him, and we will come to him and make our home with him. Whoever does not love me does not keep my words. And the word that you hear is not mine but the Father's who sent me'" (vv. 23–24). Thaddaeus might not have been very satisfied with that answer; it sounds very much like a repeat of what Jesus said in verse 21, which sounds exactly like verse 15. They all say the same thing: "If you love me, you will keep my commandments, and I will manifest myself to you."

We begin to get the idea that this is an important concept.

The point Christ made to Thaddaeus—and it is an important one—was that He would manifest Himself in a *spiritual* sense. He would reveal Himself and the Father in someone's heart, to His spiritual senses, not physically, in a way that can be seen with eyes of flesh. As we have seen, unregenerate people lack the ability to perceive or appreciate spiritual things. So the only one who can comprehend the manifestation Christ referred to is one who loves Him with a love that obeys.

In other words, *obedience is a legitimate test of whether one's love for Christ and faith in Him are real.*

It is not a question of perfection. If we say we are without sin, we call God a liar (1 John 1:10). Nor does this suggest it's possible to earn salvation with obedience. Salvation is a gift that comes by grace through faith. Obedience is the fruit of redemption, not the other way around. Forgiveness from sin cannot be earned or deserved. However, faith that does not produce obedience is not authentic saving faith (see James 2:17).

Again, the test of faith's genuineness is not *perfection,* but the *direction* of one's life. Those who truly love Christ *will* obey Him. Because we are fallen creatures with the remnants of fleshly desires and habits still vying for our affection, we do not obey perfectly. Indeed, believers sin, sometimes scandalously. Still, every true believer in his heart of hearts loves the Lord, wants to obey, and pursues sanctification. And in that regard, they are markedly different from the rest of the world.

Jesus continues in John 14:24: "Whoever does not love me does not keep my words. And the word that you hear is not mine but the Father's who sent me." Worldly and disobedient people don't want Christ. They reject His words. And since the words Jesus spoke came from the Father, the world rejects the Father, too. And He will not manifest Himself to an unbelieving, unloving, God-hating world.

Don't miss the fact that Jesus claims His words are the Father's. That is the highest claim to authority He could make. He was in essence saying, "If you reject my words, you have rejected God." What He taught is the Father's truth. Throughout His earthly ministry, Christ had surrendered His own will—His thoughts, words, ideas, attitudes, actions, and teaching—to the Father. He said, "I have come down from heaven, not to do my own will but the will of him who sent me" (John 6:38). "I always do the things that are pleasing to [the Father]" (John 8:29). "I can do nothing on my own. As I hear, I judge, and my judgment is just, because I seek not my own will but the will of him who sent me" (John 5:30).

Of course, there never was any conflict between the will of the Father and the will of Christ, but He repeatedly emphasized that fact that He was acting on the Father's authority and in accord with the Father's will, not His own, as a testimony of His absolute devotion to the Father. "I do as the Father has commanded me, so that the world may know that I love the Father" (John 14:31).

It was an expression of faithfulness, and it epitomizes the spirit of authentic faith. That's why Jesus taught the disciples that their obedience was the definitive test of their love for Him.

A SUPERNATURAL TEACHER

Throughout His earthly ministry, Jesus had spoken only the Father's words. But the disciples had frequently had trouble understanding. For example, in John 2:22 we read, "When therefore he was raised from the dead, his disciples remembered that he had said this, and they believed the Scripture and the word that Jesus had spoken." John 12:16 says, "His disciples did not understand these things at first, but when Jesus was glorified, then they remembered that these things had been written about him and had been done to him." In John 16:12, at the end of this long evening of instruction, Jesus says, "I still have many things to say to you, but you cannot bear them now." It was their last night together on earth, and the disciples were failing to grasp so much of what He was trying to tell them that He ultimately called a halt to the teaching session.

Christ was turning over the continuing instruction of these disciples to the Holy Spirit, who would dwell in them. "These things I have spoken to you while I am still with you. But the Helper, the Holy Spirit, whom the Father will send in my name, he will teach you all things and bring to your remembrance all that I have said to you" (John 14:25–26). For three years He had been teaching them the Father's truth. Yet there was so much they still did not understand. Now He would turn them over to a resident who would dwell within, to teach them and remind them continually of what they had been taught.

The Holy Spirit comes in the name of Christ. That means, of

course, that He comes in Christ's stead. Christ had come in the name of the Father. Neither the Spirit nor the Son carries on His own ministry independently. The Holy Spirit's ministry is to stand in this world in the place of Christ. He desires what Christ desires, loves what Christ loves, does what Christ would do, and thus brings glory to Christ, not to Himself.

The Father gave His truth to Christ, who gave it to the Holy Spirit, who revealed it through the apostles and preserved it in the Word of God (1 Peter 1:21). Now the Spirit illuminates the truth for us as we study what has been revealed. The Spirit receives nothing of Himself, seeks no glory of His own, and desires only to manifest the glory of Jesus Christ.

His role is that of a Teacher: "He will teach you all things and bring to your remembrance all that I have said to you" (v. 26). That does not mean, of course, that the Holy Spirit imparts to us some kind of omniscience. "All things" is used here in a relative sense. It means "all things pertaining to spiritual maturity."

The primary import of this promise is that the Holy Spirit would enable the disciples to recall the words Jesus had spoken to them so that when they recorded them as Scripture, the words would be perfect and error-free. It is a promise of divine inspiration. Can you imagine their trying, with no supernatural help, to put together a record of Jesus' words? They had to have a supernatural Teacher to record accurately Jesus' words. In addition, the Spirit would reveal new truth. Those whom God chose wrote it down, resulting in the Word of God as we have it today. To question the accuracy or the integrity of it is to deny this crucial aspect of the Spirit's role.

Biblical inerrancy is an essential aspect of the authority of God's Word. The doctrine of inerrancy is therefore a fundamental, indispensable tenet of authentic Christian faith. Those who give up the inspiration of the Bible have given up the basis of Christianity. History has repeatedly borne that out. Churches, seminaries, and denominations that have yielded ground on the issue of inspiration have opened the floodgates to rationalism, compromise, and ultimately total apostasy. How does the promise that the Holy Spirit will instruct us and bring all things to our memory apply today? The Spirit guides us in our pursuit of truth through the Word of God. He teaches us by convicting us of sin, affirming the truth in our heart, and opening our understanding to the depths of truth God has revealed. He often brings to mind appropriate verses and truths from Scripture at just the right time.

Matthew 10:19–20 is a promise to the apostles as Christ sent them on a mission to preach among the cities, but it shows how the Spirit of God works, even today: "When they deliver you over, do not be anxious how you are to speak or what you are to say, for what you are to say will be given to you in that hour. For it is not you who speak, but the Spirit of your Father speaking through you." Nothing can take the place of the Holy Spirit's work in the life of the believer. Through Him we are "heirs of God and joint heirs with Christ" (Romans 8:17), infinitely richer than all the billionaires of the world put together, because what we possess is not a passing thing. Ours is an eternal inheritance.

Paul, quoting Isaiah, wrote, "'What no eye has seen, nor ear heard, nor the heart of man imagined, what God has prepared for those who love him'—these things God has revealed to us through the Spirit. For the Spirit searches everything, even the depths of God" (1 Corinthians 2:9–10). Christians are rich beyond imagination. And the greatest treasure of all—the Holy Spirit—dwells in us and is with us forever.

Seven

—◇◆◇—

THE GIFT OF PEACE

The Hebrew Bible often uses a familiar but significant word—*sha-lom*. In its purest sense, *shalom* means "peace." The connotation is positive. That is, when someone says, "Shalom," or, "Peace unto you," it doesn't mean, "I hope you don't have any trouble"; it means, "I hope you have all the highest good coming your way."

Most people in our world don't understand peace as a positive concept. All they think of is the absence of adversity. The definition of *peace* in many languages illustrates that. For example, among the Quechua people of the central Andes region in Ecuador and Bolivia, the word used for peace literally translates, "to sit down in one's heart." For them, peace is the opposite of running around in the midst of constant anxieties. The Ch'ol people of Mexico define peace as "a quiet heart." Those may be beautiful ways to put it, but they still seem to leave us with only the negative idea that peace is the absence of care or agitation. Closer to the meaning of the Hebrew word *shalom* is the word used by the Q'eqchi' people of Guatemala, who define peace as "quiet goodness." The term they use conveys the idea of something that is active and aggressive, not just a rest in one's own heart away from troublesome circumstances.

119

The biblical concept of peace does not focus on the absence of adversity or conflict. Biblical peace is unrelated to circumstances—it is a goodness of life that is not touched by what happens on the outside. You may be in the midst of great trials, persecution, adversity, suffering, or afflictions of various kinds and still have biblical peace.

The apostle Paul famously said he could be content in any circumstance. He demonstrated that he had peace even in the jail at Philippi, because he sang and remained confident that God was being gracious to him, even when under arrest. When the opportunity arose, he communicated God's goodness to the Philippian jailer and brought him and his family to salvation.

Paul's ministerial résumé included this long litany of tribulations he had suffered:

labors . . . imprisonments, with countless beatings, and often near death. Five times I received at the hands of the Jews the forty lashes less one. Three times I was beaten with rods. Once I was stoned. Three times I was shipwrecked; a night and a day I was adrift at sea; on frequent journeys, in danger from rivers, danger from robbers, danger from my own people, danger from Gentiles, danger in the city, danger in the wilderness, danger at sea, danger from false brothers; in toil and hardship, through many a sleepless night, in hunger and thirst, often without food, in cold and exposure.

And, apart from other things, there is the daily pressure on me of my anxiety for all the churches. (2 Corinthians 11:23–28)

He even wrote, "I rejoice in my sufferings" (Colossians 1:24), and "I have suffered the loss of all things and count them as rubbish . . .

that I may know [Christ] and may share his sufferings" (Philippians 3:8–10).

Meanwhile, Paul constantly writes about peace. Every one of his epistles begins with a greeting of grace and peace. That was his standard greeting. He tells the Philippians, "Do not be anxious about anything, but in everything by prayer and supplication with thanksgiving let your requests be made known to God. And the peace of God, which surpasses all understanding, will guard your hearts and your minds in Christ Jesus" (Philippians 4:6–7). That was the very context in which he wrote, "I have learned in whatever situation I am to be content. I know how to be brought low, and I know how to abound. In any and every circumstance, I have learned the secret of facing plenty and hunger, abundance and need" (vv. 11–12).

Likewise, James wrote, "My brethren, count it all joy when you fall into various trials" (James 1:2).

Where does a person find the kind of peace that is not just the absence of trouble—but is the kind of peace that cannot be affected even by trouble, danger, or sorrow?

It is ironic, but highly significant, that what is surely the most definitive discourse on peace in all of Scripture comes from the Lord Jesus on the night before He died in agony. He knew what He was facing, but He still took time to comfort His disciples with the message of peace: "Peace I leave with you; my peace I give to you. Not as the world gives do I give to you. Let not your hearts be troubled, neither let them be afraid" (John 14:27).

The peace Jesus is speaking of enables believers to remain calm in the most wildly fearful circumstances. It enables them to hush a cry, still a riot, rejoice in pain and trial, and sing in the middle of suffering. This peace is never affected by circumstances but instead affects and even overrules every kind of adversity. It thrives in the midst of trouble.

THE NATURE OF PEACE

The New Testament speaks of two kinds of peace—the objective peace that has to do with one's relationship to God, and the subjective peace that has to do with one's experience in life.

The unregenerate person lacks peace with God. That was once true of all of us. We come into the world fighting against God, because we are a part of the rebellion that started with Adam and Eve. Romans 5:10 says we were enemies of God. We fought against God, and everything we did militated against His righteous principles.

But when we receive Jesus Christ, we cease being enemies of God—He makes a truce with us. We come over to His side, and the hostility is ended. Jesus Christ wrote the peace treaty with His blood shed at the cross. That treaty, that bond, that covenant declares the objective fact that we now are at peace with God.

That's what Paul means in Ephesians 6:15 when he calls the good news of salvation "the readiness given by the gospel of peace." The gospel is that which makes a person who was at war with God to be at peace with Him. This peace is *objective*—that is, it has nothing to do with how we feel or what we think. It is an accomplished fact.

Romans 5:1 says, "Since we have been justified by faith, we have peace with God through our Lord Jesus Christ." We who trust Christ are redeemed, totally forgiven, and declared righteous by faith. Our sins are forgiven, rebellion ceases, the war is over, and we have peace with God. Rather than being at enmity with Him, all who believe are given a standing as His adopted children. That was God's wonderful purpose in salvation.

Colossians 1:19–22 says that in Christ "all the fullness of God was pleased to dwell, and through him to reconcile to himself all things, whether on earth or in heaven, making peace by the blood of his cross.

And you, who once were alienated and hostile in mind, doing evil deeds, he has now reconciled in his body of flesh by his death, in order to present you holy and blameless and above reproach before him."

A sinful, vile, wicked individual cannot come into the presence of a holy God. Something must make that unholy person righteous before he can be at peace with God. And that's exactly what Christ did when He died for our sin and imputed His perfect righteousness to all who believe. "For our sake [God] made [Christ] to be sin who knew no sin, so that in him we might become the righteousness of God" (2 Corinthians 5:21). That is, in Pauline terminology, "the message of reconciliation" (v. 19). We are reconciled. We are at peace with God.

God was on the righteous side. We were on the opposite side. Christ atoned for our sin, imputed to us the perfect righteousness God requires, and brought us together with God, thus "making peace by the blood of his cross" (Colossians 1:20).

Whereas God and man were once estranged, they have now been reconciled. That is the heart of the gospel message. As Paul says in 2 Corinthians 5:18–19, "All this is from God, who through Christ reconciled us to himself and gave us the ministry of reconciliation; that is, in Christ God was reconciling the world to himself, not counting their trespasses against them." That is how God Himself through Christ paved the way to peace—*objective peace with God*, although we were once set in our hearts against Him, as bitter enemies.

But in John 14:27, Jesus is not talking about objective peace. The peace He speaks of there is a subjective, experiential peace. It is tranquility of the soul—a settled, positive peace that thrives regardless of life's circumstances. It is peace that is aggressive; rather than being victimized by events, it attacks them and gobbles them up. It is a supernatural, permanent, positive, no-side-effects, divine tranquilizer. This peace is the heart's calm after Calvary's storm. It is the firm conviction that "He who did not spare his own Son but gave him up for us all [will] also with him graciously give us all things" (Romans 8:32).

This is the peace of Philippians 4:7 ("the peace of God, which surpasses all understanding"). Again, this peace is impervious to adversity and conflict—unlike the world's notion of peace. So the peace of God doesn't necessarily make sense to the carnal mind. But that's only part of what Paul means when he says it "surpasses all understanding." He's saying it is a peace so profound and so powerful that it surpasses human comprehension in every sense. Even believers who experience it cannot fully understand it. It is a supernatural peace that comes from God, not a state of mind anyone can concoct on his own or stir up by sheer force of the human will. It is Christ's gift to His people.

This peace, Paul says, "will guard your hearts and your minds in Christ Jesus." The Greek term translated "guard" in that verse is not a word that means "to watch," or "keep imprisoned." It is a term with military connotations, meaning "to stand at a post and guard against the aggression of an enemy." When peace is on guard, the Christian has entered an impregnable citadel from which nothing can dislodge him. The name of the fortress is Christ, and the guard is peace. The peace of God stands guard and keeps worry from burdening our hearts. It stops unworthy thoughts from entering our minds.

That is the kind of peace we all really want (and desperately need). It is a peace that deals with the past—so that the conscience is fully cleansed and the corrosive poison of past sins is washed away. It is a peace that governs the present, with no unsatisfied desires gnawing at our hearts. It is a peace that holds promise for the future, where no foreboding fear of some dark, unknown tomorrow can threaten.

That was the peace Jesus left with His disciples. The guilt of their past had been forgiven; their present trials would all be overcome; and their destiny in the future was secured for all eternity. It was a rich and lavish gift.

THE SOURCE OF PEACE

This subjective, experiential peace (the peace *of* God) has its foundation in the objective, factual peace (peace *with* God). The peace *of* God is not obtainable by those who are not at peace *with* God. God alone can give peace. In fact, in Romans 15:33; 16:20; Philippians 4:9; 1 Thessalonians 5:23; and again in Hebrews 13:20, He is called "the God of peace."

But Jesus Christ is the One who made peace possible and through whom God's peace is given: "Peace I leave with you; my peace I give to you" (John 14:27). Notice He says *"my* peace." Here is the key to the supernatural nature of this peace: it is Jesus' own personal peace. It is the same deep, rich peace that stilled His heart in the midst of mockers, haters, murderers, traitors, and everything else He faced. He had an extraordinary calm about Him that was unlike any normal human reaction to adversity. In the midst of incomprehensible resistance and persecution, He consistently remained calm and unfaltering. It was the classic demonstration of peace that surpasses human understanding. He was a rock.

Those who knew Him might have come to expect it, but you can imagine how it must have confounded His enemies and those who didn't know Him—to see someone that calm in the face of hellish opposition. When Jesus appeared before Pilate, He was so calm, so serene, so controlled, and so at peace that Pilate became greatly disturbed. He was bewildered by Jesus and perplexed at the irrational hostility of the lynch mob. And the way Jesus stood before him in such fearless peace only added to Pilate's utter disorientation. He was accustomed to being the one in control, yet he became agitated, troubled, angry, churning with conflict. He could not conceal his own soul's disquiet. In a near frenzy, he said to Jesus, "You will not speak to me? Do you not know that I have authority to release you and authority to crucify you?" (John 19:10).

Then in perfect peace Jesus replied. "You would have no authority over me at all unless it had been given you from above" (v. 11). That's the kind of peace Jesus is talking about in John 14:27. That peace of mind is what He bequeathed to His disciples. It is undistracted fearlessness and trust. Christ is the only source of that peace.

In fact, Christ is seen throughout the New Testament as the singular dispenser of peace. In Acts 10:36, Peter preaches about "the word that [God] sent to Israel, preaching good news of peace through Jesus Christ." Second Thessalonians 3:16 says, "Now may the Lord of peace himself give you peace at all times in every way."

This is a stunning thought: Jesus Christ gives us His own personal peace. It has been tested; it was Christ's own shield and His helmet that served Him in spiritual battle. He gave it to us when He left. It should give us the same serenity in danger, the same calm in trouble, and the same freedom from anxiety.

THE GIVER OF PEACE

The Holy Spirit is the agent through whom Christ's gift of peace is dispensed to us. In Galatians 5:22, one key aspect of the fruit of the Spirit is peace. You might ask, if it was Christ's peace, why is the Holy Spirit giving it? The answer is in John 16:14, where Christ says of the Holy Spirit, "He will glorify me, for he will take what is mine and declare it to you." The Holy Spirit's ministry is to take the things of Christ and give them to His people. That, as a matter of fact, is a fair description of what the process of sanctification is all about. The Holy Spirit is conforming us to the image of Christ. As part of that process, He makes us partakers of the same peace that always kept guard over the heart and mind of Christ.

Notice that every promise Jesus made to His troubled disciples on the night before His death was rooted in the coming of the Holy Spirit. Christ promised life, union with God, full understanding, and peace to His disciples, but it is always the Spirit of God who takes the things of Christ and gives them to us.

The Contrast of Jesus' Peace and the World's Peace

In John 14:27, Jesus says. "Not as the world gives do I give to you." He is making the point emphatically that His peace is nothing whatsoever like this world's notion of peace.

The world's peace is worthless. A study made in the first decade of the new millennium revealed that "wars are becoming more frequent. More precisely, the frequency of bilateral militarized conflicts among independent states has been rising steadily over 130 years."[1] The Heidelberg Institute for International Conflict Research released figures showing that 2011 saw more armed conflict worldwide than any year since the end of World War II.[2] As a matter of fact, there has never been a time in recorded human history when the world has been truly at peace. A snapshot of the world at any time would reveal

---

1   Mark Harrison and Nicolaus Wolf, "The Frequency of Wars," University of Warwick, last modified March 10, 2011, http://www2.warwick.ac.uk/fac/soc/economics/staff/academic/harrison/public/ehr2011postprint.pdf.

2   "German researchers count record number of wars in 2011," Deutsche Welle, February 23, 2012, http://www.dw.de/german-researchers-count-record-number-of-wars-in-2011/a-15765187.

that "wars and rumors of wars" (Mark 13:7) are standard business for this cursed world.

In the summer of 2013, for example, Egypt was in turmoil, Syrian officials were allegedly waging war on their own people with chemical weapons, and a decades-old conflict was still going on in Afghanistan. While those wars were grabbing headlines, countless other conflicts we rarely heard of were simultaneously making peace impossible. A running tally at Wikipedia revealed that at least 46 armed conflicts were troubling the world at the time. At least ten of those conflicts had resulted in more than a thousand deaths.[3] An editorial that made the rounds in several American newspapers several years ago summed the situation up well: "Peace, splendid peace, is a fable, a dream, a glorious delusion. It is, without doubt, the grandest myth of them all."[4]

Humanity does not know peace. People are not even at peace in their own homes. Marriages are shattered and torn apart. There is no communication, no love, no care, and no concern. There is no peace in the heart, no peace in the family, no peace in our schools, no peace on the job, no peace in the nation, and certainly no peace in the world.

The only peace this world can know is shallow and unfulfilling. Most people's pursuit of peace is only an attempt to get away from problems. That is why people seek "peace" through alcohol, drugs, or other forms of escapism. The fact is, apart from God, there is no real peace in this world. The peace of putting your blinders on, of going to bed and forgetting it, is fleeting and worthless. And yet people try desperately to hold on to that kind of mock peace.

It is a futile pursuit. The ungodly can never know true peace.

---

3 "List of ongoing military conflicts," Wikipedia article, accessed August 22, 2013, http://en .wikipedia.org/wiki/List_of_ongoing_military_conflicts.

4 T. N. Alexakos, "Peace, Splendid Peace Is a Fable, a Dream," *Ogden Standard Examiner,* June 24, 1967, 2.

They might know only a momentary tranquility—a shallow feeling, perhaps stimulated by positive circumstances mixed with a lot of ignorance. In fact, if unsaved people knew what destiny awaited them without God, the illusory peace borne out of ignorance would evaporate instantly.

People today live in a form of existential shock. They don't understand who they are, where they are going, or what they are going to do when they get there—*if* they get there. I once saw a sign on a man's desk that said, "I've got so many troubles that if anything else happens to me, it will be two weeks before I can even worry about it."

That is a commentary on the plight of modern man. But the real truth is, the reason people today can't find peace has nothing to do with emotions or environment. If you lack peace, it is not because of your mother, your father, your grandparents, the church you were reared in, or some bad experience you had when you were a child. The Bible tells us why people don't have peace: "The heart is deceitful above all things, and desperately sick" (Jeremiah 17:9). Isaiah 48:22 says, "'There is no peace,' says the Lord, 'for the wicked.'" The human heart in its natural, fallen state is desperately wicked, and thus real peace is impossible apart from Christ.

Throughout the land of Judah in Jeremiah's day, problems were rising up fast. A great army was coming in to destroy Jerusalem and take the people into captivity, and they were frightened. God's enemies were removing peace from the land, and there was destruction coming like Judah had never experienced.

The people of Judah made a superficial effort to mend their evil ways, but it was a weak and temporary show of submission to God's commands. Nevertheless, false prophets among them were assuring the nation that everything was OK. Jeremiah 6:14 says, "They have healed the wound of my people lightly, saying, 'Peace, peace,' when there is no peace." There was a lot of talk about peace, just like today. But there was no genuine peace on the horizon. In Jeremiah 8:15, the prophet declares, "We looked for peace, but no good came; for a time of healing, but behold, terror."

A few chapters later, Jeremiah repeats the same observation: "Have you utterly rejected Judah? Does your soul loathe Zion? Why have you struck us down so that there is no healing for us? We looked for peace, but no good came; for a time of healing, but behold, terror" (14:19). Further on, the prophet puts his finger on the source of the trouble: "For thus says the Lord: Do not enter the house of mourning, or go to lament or grieve for them, for I have taken away my peace from this people, my steadfast love and mercy, declares the Lord" (16:5). Where there was unrepentant sin, there could be no true peace.

We can expect nothing different in these last days. Daniel 9:27 suggests that when the Tribulation begins there will be a brief period of peace, but after about three and a half years, peace will be taken from the earth (Revelation 6:4). Luke 21:26 says men's hearts will fail them from fear. In other words, people will be dropping dead from heart attacks caused by fear.

The world's notion of peace is a false promise—a lie that cannot satisfy. No person without Jesus Christ can ever know real peace, and no world without God can ever live in peace. If a person seems to have a moment of peace other than the peace of Jesus Christ, it is only a cynical, satanic camouflage that obscures the severity of the coming judgment.

THE RESULT OF PEACE

Jesus tells us the proper response to His promise of peace. "Let not your hearts be troubled, neither let them be afraid" (John 14:27). We who know Christ ought to be able to lay hold of His peace. It is there, it is ours, but we must receive it by faith. It is interesting that He says, "My peace I give to you," then, "Let not your hearts be troubled." His sovereign grace is revealed in the promise; our responsibility is seen in the subsequent command. The peace He gives has to be received and applied in our lives. The promise, however, is as sure as Christ Himself is faithful: if we lay hold of the promise of Christ's genuine peace, we *will* have calm, untroubled hearts, regardless of external circumstances.

If you have a troubled heart, it is because you do not believe God as you should—you do not really trust His promise of peace. Anxiety and turmoil seldom focus on present circumstances. Normally, anxiety is trouble borrowed from either the past or the future. Some people worry about things that might happen. Others' anxieties come out of remembering the past. But both the future and the past are under the care of God. He promises to supply our future need, and He has forgiven our past transgressions. Don't worry about either tomorrow or yesterday: "Sufficient for the day is its own trouble" (Matthew 6:34). But "The steadfast love of the Lord never ceases; his mercies never come to an end; they are new every morning" (Lamentations 3:22–23). So concentrate on trusting God for *today's* needs.

The peace of Christ is a great resource in helping us to know the will of God. Colossians 3:15 says, "Let the peace of Christ rule in your hearts, to which indeed you were called in one body. And be thankful." The word translated "rule" is from the Greek word *brabeuo,* which means "to umpire." Paul was urging the Colossians to let the peace of Christ be the referee in all their conflicts, decisions, and dealings with one another. In other words, "Let us pursue what makes for peace and for mutual upbuilding" (Romans 14:9). "If possible, so far as it depends on you, live peaceably with all" (12:18). "Turn away from evil and do good; seek peace and pursue it" (Psalm 34:14; 1 Peter 3:11). "Rejoice. Aim for restoration, comfort one another, agree with one another, live in peace; and the God of love and peace will be with you" (2 Corinthians 13:11). "Strive for peace with everyone, and for the holiness without which no one will see the Lord" (Hebrews 12:14).

Do you have a problem, or a decision to make? Let the peace of Christ make that decision for you. If you have examined a planned action in the light of God's Word and His Word does not forbid you from going ahead with it, if you can do it and retain the peace of Christ in your heart, do it with the confidence that it is God's will. But if you must sacrifice a sense of Christ's peace and God's blessing in order to carry out your plan, don't do it.

If a certain course of action will rob your soul of rest and peace, don't do it. "Whatever does not proceed from faith is sin" (Romans 14:23). Let Christ's peace be the umpire that makes the call.

There are two conspicuous reasons not to sin. One is that sin is an offense to the Holy God we love. He hates sin, and our love for Him should make us passionate about pleasing Him. The other reason is that sin destroys our peace, because it incurs God's displeasure and burdens our conscience with guilt.

Consider Colossians 3:15 once more. It tells us that peace is the birthright of every Christian. Paul refers to it as "the peace of Christ . . . to which indeed you were called in one body." Peace is the essential feature of genuine Christian unity. If we disregard that peace, if we refuse to let it be the umpire in our fellowship with one another, we cannot have unity in the body of Christ, for everyone will be doing his own thing and the body will be divided.

The peace of Christ is also an unending source of strength in the midst of difficulties. It is the quiet power that sustains us and enables us to endure every hardship, persecution, even death—with absolute serenity. As Stephen sank bleeding and bruised under the stones of a cursing mob, he offered a loving, forgiving prayer for his murderers: "Lord, do not hold this sin against them" (Acts 7:60). Paul was driven out of one city, dragged almost lifeless out of another, stripped by robbers, and arraigned before ruler after ruler. Yet he had an uncanny peace in all his afflictions. He wrote,

> We are afflicted in every way, but not crushed; perplexed, but not driven to despair; persecuted, but not forsaken; struck down, but not destroyed; always carrying in the body the death of Jesus, so that the life of Jesus may also be manifested in our bodies. For we who live are always being given over to death for Jesus' sake, so that the life of Jesus also may be manifested in our mortal flesh. . . .
>
> We do not lose heart. Though our outer self is wasting away, our inner self is being renewed day by day. For this light momentary affliction is preparing for us an eternal weight of glory beyond all comparison, as we look not to the things that are seen but to the things that are unseen. For the things that are seen are transient, but the things that are unseen are eternal. (2 Corinthians 4:8–11, 16–18)

At one point during Paul's imprisonment in Rome, he even had to endure abuse from fellow ministers of the gospel who for carnal, selfish reasons were actually glad to see him in distress—and preached in a way that aimed at compounding his miseries. He writes of them:

Some indeed preach Christ from envy and rivalry, but others from good will. The latter do it out of love, knowing that I am put here for the defense of the gospel. The former proclaim Christ out of rivalry, not sincerely but thinking to afflict me in my imprisonment.

What then? Only that in every way, whether in pretense or in truth, Christ is proclaimed, and in that I rejoice. Yes, and I will rejoice, for I know that through your prayers and the help of the Spirit of Jesus Christ this will turn out for my deliverance, as it is my eager expectation and hope that I will not be at all ashamed, but that with full courage now as always Christ will be honored in my body, whether by life or by death. (Philippians 1:15–20)

That exemplifies the peace of Christ—the same kind of peace with which He "endured the cross, despising the shame" (Hebrews 12:2). Paul didn't focus on his problems, but on the promises of God to sustain and ultimately glorify him.

Trouble comes and goes, but glory is eternal. Paul understood that, and that's why in the midst of his trials he could write, "Rejoice in the Lord always; again I will say, Rejoice" (Philippians 4:4).

To have that supernatural peace available puts us under obligation to lean on it. Colossians 3:15 is not a command to *seek* peace, but rather a plea to let the Lord's peace work in us, to let it rule in our hearts. The peace of Christ is yours. Now let it rule. Perfect peace comes when our focus is *off* the problem, *off* the trouble, and constantly *on* Christ. Isaiah 26:3 says, "You keep him in perfect peace whose mind is stayed on you, because he trusts in you."

In the midst of a society where we are constantly bombarded with advertising and other worldly pressures designed to get us to focus on our needs and problems, how can we keep our minds focused on Christ? By studying the Word of God and allowing the Holy Spirit to teach us—by permitting Him to fix our hearts on the person of Jesus Christ. That, after all, is the Holy Spirit's unique work. In Jesus' words: "He will glorify me, for he will take what is mine and declare it to you."

Eight

WHAT JESUS' DEATH MEANT TO HIM

As we look back on the cross after almost two thousand years, we stand in awe at all that God through Jesus Christ accomplished there for us. At the cross the very Son of God suffered shame and ridicule at the hands of wicked, murdering men. He did it willingly to provide forgiveness for our sins and access to God. God's justice was perfectly fulfilled. The penalty we owed was paid in full by Christ. God's judgment against us was thus stayed and the righteousness of Christ became ours. The Father set us free to commune with Him, and we became His children and objects of His love.

When the disciples looked forward to the cross, they could only wonder what it meant. They had been with Jesus for three blessed years during which He had loved them and supplied all their needs. When they heard Him talk about His death, they found it impossible to understand. How could God incarnate die, and what would life be like without their beloved Master and Teacher? Paralyzing fear must have come over them at the mere thought of it. And then when they realized the time was at hand, the anticipation of loneliness set in. Looking ahead on that awful night before He died, they could see nothing but the oppressive specter of tragedy.

The problem was the disciples' faulty perspective; they were looking at Christ's death from their own viewpoint—they gave little thought to what it meant to Him. Their faith was weak, but beyond that they had a simple problem: selfishness. They wanted Jesus to stay with them because He loved them and took care of them. In a sense, they were thinking just like the multitudes who followed Jesus as long as He fed them, but who didn't want to pay the price of following Him wholeheartedly. They were moping around, brooding, stewing over their own dilemma, thinking only of how Jesus' death would affect *their* problems, *their* expectations, *their* hopes, *their* ambitions, and *their* desires. Their love was too superficial in that it was based on a desire for their own good, not on a desire for the will of the One they loved.

We tend to respond that same way when death touches us. We feel great sorrow, but often for the wrong reasons. We may wonder why God would take our loved one—as if we should have some guaranteed amount of time on earth together. When a Christian dies, sorrow is normal for a while, and tears can be healthy. We grieve, but not like those who have no hope (1 Thessalonians 4:13). When sorrow continues unabated or overwhelms the heart with despair, it may be because the grieving person is seeing the loss from a selfish perspective rather than from the departed believer's viewpoint. We must see a Christian's death from the right perspective. It means ultimate release from the body of sin, abiding bliss, unending joy, and an unfettered view of God's eternal glory.

Jesus' death, on the other hand, was not release from a body of sin, but virtually the opposite. His sinless body was ravaged by the curse of sin. He was bearing a world of sins—the guilt of His people. And before He could enter into unending joy, He would face the dreadful weight of God's infinite wrath against sin. It would be poured out on His sinless head in full measure, as a payment to atone for the transgressions of all His people of all time. In those mysterious hours He suffered more agony than you and I could ever begin to imagine, much less endure. But He emerged triumphant, and was glorified in the process.

He anticipated it all with a willing heart, knowing it was the Father's will and eager to obey. As the cross drew near, He revealed to His disciples what it meant to Him:

> You heard me say to you, "I am going away, and I will come to you." If you loved me, you would have rejoiced, because I am going to the Father, for the Father is greater than I. And now I have told you before it takes place, so that when it does take place you may believe. I will no longer talk much with you, for the ruler of this world is coming. He has no claim on me, but I do as the Father has commanded me, so that the world may know that I love the Father.
>
> Rise, let us go from here. (John 14:28–31)

The disciples naturally viewed Jesus' death with sorrow, but to Him it meant joy. "For the joy that was set before him [he] endured the cross" (Hebrews 12:2). The disciples' sorrow is certainly normal and understandable. It seems a bit of a jolt for Jesus to say, "If you loved me, you would have rejoiced." No righteous person could ever contemplate Jesus' sufferings with any kind of delight. But His point is that if they had been more attentive to Him and less obsessed with their own sorrow—if they had loved Him as they should—they might have learned the reasons for His joy and found a way to rejoice with

Him. After all, four marvelous, eternal triumphs were going to be won at the cross.[1]

THE PERSON OF CHRIST WOULD BE DIGNIFIED

Bear in mind that before the incarnation, Jesus had always existed in the utter perfection of eternal glory. He experienced the Father's infinite love and fellowship with a perfection and intensity that is impossible for us to comprehend. But He left His glory behind when He came to earth. He came not as a king to a magnificent palace, but as a tiny baby born in a drab, humble stable. He lived by modest means; He had no regular place to lay His head. He suffered the hatred, abuse, and jeers of evil men. He was rejected by His own people and vilified even by the religious leaders. "He was despised and rejected by men; a man of sorrows, and acquainted with grief; and as one from whom men hide their faces he was despised, and we esteemed him not" (Isaiah 53:3).

From our human perspective, one of the most incomprehensible truths about Jesus Christ is that He, the eternal Lord of Glory, was willing to humble Himself so completely for our sakes. He stepped down from a position of equality with the Most High God and condescended to share His riches with us. Second Corinthians 8:9 says, "You know the grace of our Lord Jesus Christ, that though he was rich, yet for your sake he became poor, so that you by his poverty might become rich." Jesus had all the riches of heaven, yet He gave them up for a while so we could share them with Him forever. Here's how Scripture further explains Jesus' condescension:

---

1 For an extensive study of the drama and significance of Christ's death, see John MacArthur, *The Murder of Jesus* (Nashville: Word, 2000).

But we see him who for a little while was made lower than the angels, namely Jesus, crowned with glory and honor because of the suffering of death, so that by the grace of God he might taste death for everyone. . . . Therefore he had to be made like his brothers in every respect, so that he might become a merciful and faithful high priest in the service of God, to make propitiation for the sins of the people. For because he himself has suffered when tempted, he is able to help those who are being tempted. (Hebrews 2:9, 17–18)

Jesus became one of us. He suffered what we suffer, not only so He could redeem us, but also so He could sympathize with us. The incarnation allowed Him to experience all the temptations, difficulties, griefs, and heartbreaks of His people. He can empathize with us; from His own experience He understands our struggles. "We do not have a high priest who is unable to sympathize with our weaknesses, but one who in every respect has been tempted as we are, yet without sin" (Hebrews 4:15).

Philippians 2:6–10 describes the incarnation as an act of unselfish humility by Jesus, "who, though he was in the form of God, did not count equality with God a thing to be grasped" (v. 6). Equality with God was indeed His by divine right to hold on to, but He did not covet the privileges and prerogatives of His own deity when the redemption of His people was at stake. Instead, He "made himself nothing, taking the form of a servant, being born in the likeness of men. And being found in human form, he humbled himself by becoming obedient to the point of death, even death on a cross" (vv. 7–8). He was willing to come down to earth and become a servant, even knowing that it meant death on a cross.

Because the Son humbly obeyed, the Father exalted Him. Paul

continues, "Therefore God has highly exalted him and bestowed on him the name that is above every name, so that at the name of Jesus every knee should bow, in heaven and on earth and under the earth, and every tongue confess that Jesus Christ is Lord, to the glory of God the Father" (vv. 9–10).

There have always been those who get confused about the humiliation of Christ. They think that because He humbled Himself and became a servant, they are not to worship Him as God. Actually, the opposite is true. Because He humbled Himself, He is to be exalted to the uttermost. Every knee will ultimately bow before Him and confess that Jesus Christ is Lord.

Arians, gnostics, Jehovah's Witnesses, Unitarians, Socinians, modernists, and others who with an agenda deny the deity of Christ have often twisted the meaning of John 14:28, trying to turn it into proof that Jesus is inferior to the Father. When He said, "the Father is greater than I," He referred not to His essential being, but to His role as a humbled servant. While He was humbled, the Father was in glory and therefore in a greater place of honor. Jesus put Himself beneath the Father's glory. He also subjugated His will to the Father's will. In the Garden of Gethsemane, He prayed to the Father: "Remove this cup from me. Yet not what I will, but what you will" (Mark 14:36). Jesus repeatedly claimed to be equal in deity to the Father. We have already seen one significant example of that in John 14:9. When Philip asked to be shown the Father, Jesus answered, "Whoever has seen me has seen the Father." He took on a *role* that was beneath the Father, but He was not inferior in nature or essence (cf. Titus 2:13).

At the end of His earthly ministry, as He approached the cross, knowing what lay ahead of Him, Christ knelt prior to entering the Garden of Gethsemane and prayed to the Father: "I glorified you on earth, having accomplished the work that you gave me to do. And now, Father, glorify me in your own presence with the glory that I had with you before the world existed" (John 17:4–5).

Jesus was looking ahead to the full expression of His glory—that same pristine glory He knew before the humiliation of His incarnation. Our Savior found joy as He approached the cross because He knew that on the other side of His sufferings He would be restored to the full expression of deity. He looked forward to it and wanted His beloved friends to share His joy. "If you loved me, you would have rejoiced, because I am going to the Father, for the Father is greater than I" (John 14:28).

Occasionally I meet someone who thinks the crucifixion was a surprise and at least a temporary defeat for Jesus—as if He didn't know ahead of time how much He would suffer. He knew. He was familiar with the prophecies of Isaiah 53 and Psalm 22, both of which contain detailed accounts of the crucifixion—written long before Christ's birth. Certainly He knew what He had come for. Long before going to Jerusalem to die, He told the disciples, "I have a baptism to be baptized with, and how great is my distress until it is accomplished!" (Luke 12:50). The crucifixion was not an afterthought, but a crucial element in the plan of God from before the beginning of time. Our Lord knew exactly what was going to happen, but He went to the cross anyway.

It was a bitter cup, but He was willing to drink it.

THE TRUTH WOULD BE DOCUMENTED

Jesus had made many claims about Himself to the disciples. Although they wanted to believe those claims—and for the most part they did—doubt would often creep into their hearts. They found much of Jesus' teaching about who He was and why He came difficult to fathom. So they sometimes teetered between belief and uncertainty.

Jesus used a simple method to strengthen their faith—He would predict events. When what He said happened, the disciples would remember what He had predicted. One prophecy after another came true, and each fulfillment grounded their faith a little more. By the day of Pentecost, their faith was so strong that they fearlessly proclaimed the gospel to thousands of pilgrims gathered in Jerusalem for the festival.

Jesus acknowledged this use of prediction to strengthen their faith: "I have told you before it takes place, so that when it does take place you may believe" (John 14:29). He knew the eleven didn't fully believe everything yet, but their faith would be unshakable when His words came true. Fulfilled prophecy is perhaps the greatest proof that the Word of God is true. Only a determined unbeliever, someone with an agenda to reject the truth no matter what, can dismiss the fulfilled prophecies of Psalm 22 and Isaiah 53 as insignificant evidence of the Bible's authority.

Once I was talking to a man who said that Israel no longer has a place in the plan of God. I pointed out that Scripture prophesied that Israel would be regathered in the land—just the way we see it happening today. Then I asked him, "What does your theology do with that?" He replied, "It wiggles a lot." Fulfilled prophecy has a devastating way of dealing with human doubt.

In John 13:19 Jesus used the same method to strengthen the disciples' faith: "I am telling you this now, before it takes place, that when it does take place you may believe that I am he." As we noted in an earlier chapter, there is a deep significance in His words at the end of that verse. The English translators added the pronoun "he." What Jesus actually said was, "believe that I am"—using the well-known name by which God identified Himself to Moses at the burning bush. What He wanted to validate and seal was their faith in Him *as God*.

Specifically, that verse is referring to Jesus' prediction that Judas

Iscariot was going to betray Him. "The Scripture will be fulfilled, 'He who ate my bread has lifted his heel against me'" (John 13:18). You can imagine what they thought later when they saw Judas betray Jesus in the garden. Their minds must have flashed back to what He had said earlier in the upper room. He had given them a string of prophecies and promises that began with His betrayal by Judas and ended with the promise of a divine Helper. Beginning with the betrayal in the garden, everything Jesus said came true, one by one. The disciples' faith was completely solidified by the time that last promise was fulfilled on the day of Pentecost.

The final promise to send a divine Helper was linked with the promise of supernatural peace. When the Holy Spirit descended at Pentecost, a supernatural peace like nothing the apostles had ever known flooded their hearts as the Spirit of God took residence within them. Later, when Peter and John preached, the religious authorities confronted them and ordered them to stop. They calmly responded, "Whether it is right in the sight of God to listen to you rather than to God, you must judge, for we cannot but speak of what we have seen and heard" (Acts 4:19–20).

One by one, every promise Jesus gave the disciples came to pass. With each one, their faith was further strengthened so that they trusted Him more and more. The fulfilled prophecies fully documented the truth that He was God.

You may wonder why if Jesus wanted to strengthen His men He didn't simply stay on earth and continue teaching them. The reason is that He had other, more urgent, work to do. It was time to fulfill God's purpose in redemption by atoning for sin, to depart and let the Holy Spirit do His work, and to unleash the disciples to fulfill their calling.

The events that followed did indeed strengthen the disciples' faith.

Christ said He would die on a cross, and He did. He said He would rise, and He did. He said He would ascend to the Father, and they saw Him ascend. He said the Spirit would come, and it happened. He said He would supply supernatural life, and they got it. He promised them a supernatural union with the living God, and they experienced it. He promised them an indwelling Teacher, and they received the Spirit of God. He promised them peace, and they were flooded with peace. Every detail of each prophecy came to pass just as He had said. Through those events, the disciples' faith became rock solid. His words were thus documented and their faith cemented.

The Lord's leaving was really an act of love toward the disciples. He knew their faith would have to be strong if they were to carry His message to the world. They would have to move into the full blast of Satan's fire, into the furnace of hell's opposition. Seeing all His prophecies fulfilled one after another was the best way their faith could remain strong enough for that mission.

In fact, Jesus said that if they really loved Him—if they really wanted the world to hear the gospel—they would rejoice that He was leaving. In effect He was saying, "Stop looking at My death from your own perspective and look at it from My perspective. When I go, your faith will be strengthened because the truth will be fully, irrefutably documented for you. Then you will take My message into all the world. But the longer I stay, the longer that proclamation will be postponed."

JESUS' ARCHENEMY WOULD BE DEFEATED

When Jesus came to earth, His central purpose was to redeem all who place their trust in Him. The Fall had ruined humanity's fellowship with God. Because of Adam's sin, all his offspring were born in a state of sin and rebellion—guilty, spiritually isolated, lost, in bondage to sin, and doomed. They had no communion with God and no ability to please Him or merit His favor (Romans 8:8). Christ was determined (even before the foundation of the world) to come to earth to bring fallen sinners back to God (cf. Revelation 13:8). In order to succeed, the Lord had to defeat Satan decisively. In John 14:30, Jesus informs the disciples about the coming showdown with His fiendish foe: "I will no longer talk much with you, for the ruler of this world is coming. He has no claim on me." Notice that He calls the Devil "the ruler of this world," because this world is Satan's domain and the system of evil under which this world is oppressed is of Satan's devising.

Satan was already indwelling Judas, pushing him toward the garden, where he would betray Jesus. Jesus knew that Satan was coming in the person of Judas to take Him. He knew He was about to enter the dreaded death battle with His enemy.

Jesus had resisted and overcome Satan all through His earthly life. The Devil had tried to kill Him as an infant—he had caused all the male babies to be slain throughout the region where Jesus was born (Matthew 2:16). Although the Bible is largely silent regarding the first thirty years of Jesus' life, He undoubtedly faced satanic opposition at every turn. Then when Jesus began His ministry, Satan immediately met Him in the wilderness to tempt Him. He even tried to get Jesus to bow and worship him. During Jesus' ministry, Satan tried everything. He confronted the Lord with people who hated Him and tried to kill Him, and with demons who opposed Him and tried to stop His work.

From the night of Jesus' birth to the night of His death, Satan fought against Him. Finally, His death would resolve the age-old conflict that had raged since Lucifer's fall from heaven (cf. Isaiah 14:12–15 and Ezekiel 28:12–19). The outcome would be decided at Calvary. Jesus was about to win the ultimate victory.

He had always looked forward to victory over Satan. Earlier, Jesus had declared, "Now is the judgment of this world; now will the ruler of this world be cast out. And I, when I am lifted up from the earth, will draw all people to myself" (John 12:31–32). The apostle John adds this editorial note: "He said this to show by what kind of death he was going to die" (v. 33). In other words, our Lord was saying that the ultimate defeat of Satan would be accomplished when He was "lifted up" on the cross. He went to the cross knowing it was the final blow that would wipe out Satan's power.

While Jesus was in the garden, the soldiers arrived. He asked them, "Have you come out as against a robber, with swords and clubs? When I was with you day after day in the temple, you did not lay hands on me. But this is your hour, and the power of darkness" (Luke 22:52–53). The phrase "the power of darkness" is a reference to Satan. Jesus was saying, "This is the hour for my judgment on you and the devil who has motivated you." He regarded His ordeal at the cross as a conflict with Satan. Satan would bruise Jesus on the heel, but Jesus would crush Satan's head (cf. Genesis 3:15). Christ became a man with the express purpose of destroying the Devil. Hebrews 2:14 says, "Since therefore the children [those whom Jesus came to save] share in flesh and blood, he himself likewise partook of the same things, that through death he might destroy the one who has the power of death, that is, the devil." First John 3:8 says, "The reason the Son of God appeared was to destroy the works of the devil." Jesus looked at the cross as a conflict with the Devil, and He knew He would be victorious.

Since the cross, the power of Satan has been broken. He is still active, but Christ's death and resurrection have effectively weakened him. Because he has already had his main strength broken, the Devil has no power in your life unless you yield to him. Now he is the prisoner of Christ and one day will be cast into the lake of fire.

So in effect Jesus was saying to His disciples, "Look at the cross from My perspective. I am through with this endless conflict against Satan; I've had enough of his opposition. When I go to the cross, I'm going to destroy the Devil. You shouldn't grieve, but be joyful. I'm going to defeat the archenemy who has troubled us for ages." It turned out that all of Satan's schemes to get Jesus to the cross were only part of God's plan to destroy His enemy.

Satan tried desperately but in vain to find a place where Jesus was vulnerable. Jesus says in John 14:30, "The ruler of this world . . . has no claim on me." Satan had looked for some sinful weakness in Him, but he couldn't find one because Jesus had none.

If Satan had been able to find any sin in Christ, our Lord would have been worthy of death. As Romans 6:23 says, "The wages of sin is death." But Jesus "committed no sin, neither was deceit found in his mouth" (1 Peter 2:22). He is "holy, innocent, unstained, separated from sinners, and exalted above the heavens" (Hebrews 7:26). He did not sin; He could not sin. Satan had entered into conflict with One who was not vulnerable. It was Satan who would be destroyed.

LOVE WOULD BE DEMONSTRATED

If Jesus did nothing to deserve death, we are left wondering why He was allowed to die. The answer is that Jesus wanted to demonstrate His love for the Father. He was voluntarily going to the cross "so that the world may know that I love the Father" (John 14:31). As a Son, He was obedient to His Father. While it is also true that He died to demonstrate His love for His people, here He emphasizes His love for *the Father.* It was a supreme act of love for Him to die in accordance with His Father's will.

It is interesting that although Jesus often spoke of His *obedience* to the Father, this is the only time in the New Testament He specifically affirms His *love* for the Father. But remember the point Jesus Himself made in John 14:15: Obedience is the fruit of authentic love. So each mention of His obedience to the Father implies love as well.

The religious leaders of Jesus' day all claimed to love God. But theirs was a superficial imitation of love, and it couldn't pass the test of obedience. This is an important point throughout Jesus' discourse. He had already said three times emphatically that the test of true love is obedience (John 14:15, 21, 23). Now He was going to give the disciples living proof of His love for God; He would die because that was the Father's plan. He would die because He loved the Father—not because He deserved death, but because God had designed it for the redemption of sinners. Jesus wanted to show the world His love for the Father, and He rejoiced at the opportunity, for love is shown best in selfless, sacrificial service for the one loved.

You would think that as His disciples listened and learned what Jesus' death meant to Him, they would surely be jolted out of their selfish stupor. Difficult days lay ahead for them, and their pain might have been greatly eased if they could only begin to see through Jesus' eyes. He certainly wanted them to understand the grandeur of the plan of salvation that was unfolding all around them. He was certainly sending them the message with sufficient volume and clarity. If only they had listened, they might have been able to perceive beyond their selfish sense of sorrow and loneliness. But that didn't happen until after the resurrection.

Let's not think too critically of the disciples, because we are just like them—too concerned about our own problems and needs to hear

Christ. Many times our prayers are full of asking but void of thanks. We beg but don't praise. Instead of looking at things selfishly—how they affect us—we should look at the way things affect the cause of Christ. We must pray that God will cure us of ourselves so we can be totally obedient to Him.

Nine

———◇◇◇———

THE VINE
AND THE BRANCHES

A t key points in His ministry, Christ emphasized His equality with God in the clearest possible terminology. We've already taken note of one of those, in John 13:19 ("I am telling you this now, before it takes place, that when it does take place you may believe that I am"). Many of the strongest affirmations of His deity employed the same name God used when He first revealed Himself to Moses—"I am" (Exodus 3:14).

Prior to the Upper Room Discourse, Jesus had already taught the disciples, "I am the bread of life" (John 6:35); "I am the light of the world" (8:12); "I am the door" (10:9); "I am the good shepherd" (vv. 11, 14); and, "I am the way, and the truth, and the life" (14:6). All of those were clear claims of deity. Each one of them had some reference to an important attribute of God (e.g., light, truth) or an Old Testament picture of God (the Good Shepherd and the bread that comes down from heaven). There was no mistaking His intent. He was declaring that He is God.

Now He says, "I am the true vine" (15:1). Like all the other great "I am" passages recorded in the Gospel of John, this figure of speech points to His deity. Each one is a metaphor that elevates Christ to the level of Creator, Sustainer, Savior, or Lord—titles that can legitimately be claimed only by God.

> I am the true vine, and my Father is the vinedresser. Every branch in me that does not bear fruit he takes away, and every branch that does bear fruit he prunes, that it may bear more fruit. Already you are clean because of the word that I have spoken to you. Abide in me, and I in you. As the branch cannot bear fruit by itself, unless it abides in the vine, neither can you, unless you abide in me. I am the vine; you are the branches. Whoever abides in me and I in him, he it is that bears much fruit, for apart from me you can do nothing. If anyone does not abide in me he is thrown away like a branch and withers; and the branches are gathered, thrown into the fire, and burned. If you abide in me, and my words abide in you, ask whatever you wish, and it will be done for you. By this my Father is glorified, that you bear much fruit and so prove to be my disciples. (John 15:1–8)

The metaphor in this passage pictures a central vine with many branches. The vine is the source and sustenance of life for the branches, and the branches must abide in the vine to live and bear fruit. Jesus, of course, is the vine, and the branches are disciples. While it is obvious the fruit-bearing branches represent true believers, the identity of the fruitless ones is in question. Some commentators say the barren branches are redeemed people—barren or carnal Christians. Others believe the fruitless branches represent unbelievers. As always, we must look to the context for the answer.

The true meaning of the metaphor becomes clear when we consider the characters in that night's drama. The disciples were with

Jesus. He had loved them to the uttermost; He had comforted them with the words recorded in John 14. The Father was foremost in His thoughts, because He was thinking of the events surrounding His death, which would occur the next day. But Jesus was also aware of someone else—the betrayer. Only a short time before, Christ had dismissed Judas Iscariot from the fellowship because Judas rejected Jesus' final appeal of love.

All the characters of the drama were thus in the mind of Jesus. He was engaged in this teaching session with *the eleven,* whom He loved deeply and passionately. He was on His way to the garden to pray to *the Father,* with whom He had constant communion and shared an infinite love. And He was still grieving over *Judas,* who had just ended His fellowship with Jesus and the other disciples because Judas had a traitor's heart and was determined to betray Jesus for a handful of filthy lucre.

Each of those characters played a part in Jesus' metaphor. The vine is Christ; the vinedresser is the Father. The fruit-bearing branches represent the eleven and all true disciples of the church age. The fruitless branches represent Judas and all those who never were true disciples.

Jesus had long been aware of the difference between Judas and the eleven. Remember what He said after washing the disciples' feet: "you are clean, but not every one of you" (John 13:10). The apostle adds, "For he knew who was to betray him; that was why he said, 'Not all of you are clean'" (v. 11). Judas was the exception. He had never been "bathed"—"cleansed . . . by the washing of water with the word" (Ephesians 5:26). He had never submitted to "the washing of regeneration and renewal of the Holy Spirit" (Titus 3:5). He was not a regenerate man—and Jesus knew it.

As we saw in chapter 2 of our study, to the casual observer—even to the inner circle of disciples—Judas appeared to be like the others.

He was with Jesus for the same amount of time. He was so trusted that they had even delegated to him the responsibility of keeping the group's money. He looked to all the world like a true branch on the vine. There was only one difference between Judas and the other disciples: he would never bear any real spiritual fruit. So God removed Judas's branch from the vine, and it was burned.

Some would say Judas was a believer who turned away and lost his salvation. According to them, the same could happen to any believer who becomes barren of fruit. But Jesus made a promise to His redeemed ones: "I give them eternal life, and they will never perish, and no one will snatch them out of my hand" (John 10:28). He guaranteed the absolute security of every true child of God: "All that the Father gives me will come to me, and whoever comes to me I will never cast out" (John 6:37). A genuine believer cannot lose salvation and be condemned to hell. That would invalidate the promise of Christ and be a breach of His faithfulness.

A branch that is truly and intimately connected to the vine is fruitful and secure and will never be removed. But those that have only a superficial attachment—branches that are not truly tapped into the vascular system of the vine—will be removed. Most of these are shoots attached to other branches, drawing strength from them instead of from the vine itself. Some of them are attached to the very base of the central vine, but their energy is not invested in the production of fruit. Instead, they set down roots of their own. Horticulturists call these shoots "suckers." They are parasitical, and they sap vitality from the true branches. I refer to them as Judas-branches. They make an excellent metaphor for the danger Jesus is warning about.

There are people who, like Judas, appear by human perception to be united with Christ, but they are apostates doomed to hell. They may attend church, know all the right answers, speak the jargon fluently, and go through all the standard religious motions; but God will remove them, and they will be burned.

Others, like the eleven, are closely and fruitfully connected to the vine. They bear genuine fruit.

Those are the basics of this metaphor. Let's consider the particulars.

CHRIST IS THE TRUE VINE

Jesus was not introducing a new idea by using the metaphor of a vine and its branches. In the Old Testament, the people of Israel were pictured as the Lord's vine. He used them to accomplish His purpose in the world, and He blessed those connected with them. He was the vinedresser; He cared for the vine, trimmed it, and cut off branches that didn't bear fruit. But God's vine degenerated and bore no fruit. The vinedresser was deeply grieved over the tragedy of Israel's fruitlessness:

> Let me sing for my beloved my love song concerning his vineyard: My beloved had a vineyard on a very fertile hill. He dug it and cleared it of stones, and planted it with choice vines; he built a watchtower in the midst of it, and hewed out a wine vat in it; and he looked for it to yield grapes, but it yielded wild grapes. And now, O inhabitants of Jerusalem and men of Judah, judge between me and my vineyard. What more was there to do for my vineyard, that I have not done in it? When I looked for it to yield grapes, why did it yield wild grapes? And now I will tell you what I will do to my vineyard. I will remove its hedge, and it shall be devoured; I will break down its wall, and it shall be trampled down. I will make it a waste; it shall not be pruned or hoed, and briers and thorns shall grow up; I

will also command the clouds that they rain no rain upon it. For the vineyard of the Lord of hosts is the house of Israel, and the men of Judah are his pleasant planting. (Isaiah 5:1–7)

God had done everything to create a fruit-producing environment, yet Israel was spiritually barren. So He took away its wall and left it unprotected.

Foreign nations then trampled down the nation and laid it waste. Israel was no longer God's vine; it had forfeited its privilege. Now there is a new vine. No longer does blessing come through a covenantal relationship with Israel. Fruit and blessing come through a spiritual connection with Jesus Christ.

Jesus is the true vine in Scripture. The word *true* is often used by New Testament authors to describe what is eternal, heavenly, and divine. Israel was imperfect, but Christ is perfect; Israel was the type, but Christ is the reality. He is also called the true tabernacle ("the true tent that the Lord set up, not man"), as opposed to the original, earthly tabernacle (Hebrews 8:2). He is the true Light (John 1:9). God had revealed much truth in the Old Testament, but Christ is the living embodiment of truth and the full revelation of God to humanity—"The true light, which enlightens everyone." He is also the true Bread (John 6:32). God had sustained men by manna from heaven, but Christ is the real sustainer of life; the manna in the wilderness was merely a symbol of Him.

Jesus chose the figure of a vine for several reasons. The lowliness of a vine demonstrates His humility. The figure also pictures a close, permanent, vital union between Christ and His followers. It is symbolic of belonging, because branches belong entirely to the vine. If branches are to live and bear fruit, they must completely depend on the vine for nourishment, support, strength, and vitality.

Yet many who call themselves Christians fail to depend on Christ. Instead of being attached to the true vine, they are tied to a bank account. Others are attached to their education. Some draw their energy and motivation from popularity, fame, personal skills, possessions, relationships, or fleshly desires. Some think the earthly church is their vine, and they try to attach themselves to a religious system. But none of those things can sustain people for eternity and produce spiritual fruit. The only true vine is Christ.

THE FATHER IS THE VINEDRESSER

In the metaphor, Christ is a plant, but the Father is a person. Certain false teachers have claimed that it therefore shows Christ is not divine, but lower in character and essence than the Father. They say if He is God, His and the Father's parts in the metaphor should be equal. He should be the vine, and the Father should be the root of the vine. But to make such a claim is to miss the whole point of Jesus' metaphor and the reason the apostle John included it in his gospel.

While He is affirming His equality in essence with the Father—by claiming to be the Source and Sustainer of life—Jesus is also emphasizing the fundamental difference between His role and the Father's. The point is that the Father cares for the Son and for those joined to the Son by faith.

The disciples were familiar with the role of the vinedresser. After a vine is planted, the vinedresser has two duties. First, he cuts off fruitless branches, which take away sap from the fruit-bearing branches. If sap is wasted, the plant will bear less fruit. Then, he constantly trims shoots from the fruit-bearing branches so that all the sap is concentrated on fruit bearing. Jesus applies those activities to the spiritual realm: "Every branch in me that does not bear fruit he takes away, and every branch that does bear fruit he prunes, that it may bear more fruit" (John 15:2).

The fruitless branches that are cut off are useless. Since they do not burn well, they cannot even be used to warm a house. They are thrown into piles and burned like garbage. As verse 2 says, God "takes away" such branches. He doesn't repair them; He removes them.

Those who are removed never had a vital connection to the vine in the first place. Like Judas, they don't really abide in the vine. The only connection was superficial. They never had a true, life-giving, fruit-producing connection with Christ and therefore were never really saved. At some point, the Father removes them to preserve the life and fruitfulness of the other branches.

The Father prunes the fruit-bearing branches so they will bear more fruit. We know these branches represent Christians, because only Christians can bear fruit. Pruning is not done only once—it is a constant process. After continual pruning, a branch bears much fruit. "By this my Father is glorified, that you bear much fruit and so prove to be my disciples" (John 15:8).

THE FATHER REMOVES THE FRUITLESS BRANCHES

Fruit-bearing and non-fruit-bearing branches grow rapidly, and the vinedresser must carefully prune the former and remove the latter. He must know the difference. If there is to be a large quantity of fruit, every shoot that grows on the fruit-bearing branches must be cut off, lest it drain sap, sunlight, and nourishment from the fruit-bearing process.

In the first-century Middle East, it was common to prevent a vine from bearing any fruit at all for three years after it was planted. All the resources for growth went into the development of the vine itself. By the fourth year it was strong enough to bear an abundance of fruit. The careful pruning actually increased its fruit-bearing capacity. Mature branches, which had already been through the four-year process, were pruned annually between December and January.

Jesus said His followers were like mature branches that bore fruit but needed pruning. There is no such thing as a fruitless Christian. Every Christian bears some fruit. You sometimes may have to look hard to find even a small grape, but if you look diligently enough, you will find something, if you are indeed dealing with a true branch.

It is the essence of the Christian life to bear fruit. Ephesians 2:10 says, "We are his workmanship, created in Christ Jesus for good works, which God prepared beforehand, that we should walk in them." The inevitable fruit of God's grace at work in a life is an abundance of good works. James 2:17 explains the close relationship between faith and works: "Faith by itself, if it does not have works, is dead." If someone is connected to Christ with legitimate saving faith, that faith *will* produce fruit. If a person's profession of faith is a sham or his interest in Christ is merely superficial (as opposed to a wholehearted commitment of love and trust), that person will not bear any lasting fruit, but will eventually fall away and abandon his or her confession.

That does not mean works save a person, but works are evidence that faith is genuine. Jesus Himself says in John 15:8 that fruit bearing is the necessary proof of genuine discipleship.

Jesus said elsewhere as well that a genuine believer can be tested by his fruit. "You will recognize them by their fruits. Are grapes gathered from thornbushes, or figs from thistles? So, every healthy tree bears good fruit, but the diseased tree bears bad fruit. A healthy tree cannot bear bad fruit, nor can a diseased tree bear good fruit. Every tree that does not bear good fruit is cut down and thrown into the fire. Thus you will recognize them by their fruits" (Matthew 7:16–20). Jesus' illustration would make no sense whatsoever if every Christian did not bear at least some fruit.

John the Baptist recognized the connection between salvation and fruit bearing. When he saw the Pharisees and Sadducees coming to be baptized, he said, "You brood of vipers! Who warned you to flee from the wrath to come? Bear fruit in keeping with repentance" (Matthew 3:7–8). A total lack of genuine fruit showed that their repentance was not genuine.

Since all Christians bear fruit, it is clear that the fruitless branches in John 15 cannot refer to them. In fact, the fruitless branches had to be eliminated and thrown into the fire. Yet, in verse 2, Jesus refers to the fruitless branches as those who are "in me." If they are "in him," are they not genuine believers?

Not necessarily. Other passages in Scripture show it is possible to be a spiritual parasite who has the appearance of spiritual life without really being a true believer. For example, Romans 9:6 says, "Not all who are descended from Israel belong to Israel." A person can be part of the nation of Israel yet not be a true Israelite. Likewise, one can be in the vine without having a vital, abiding connection. In a similar metaphor, Romans 11:17–24 represents Israel as an olive tree from which God has removed branches. Those branches were cut off because of unbelief (v. 20).

Luke 8:18 is one of many warnings in Scripture targeting those who cultivate the appearance of godliness without any vital connection to the life of God: "Take care then how you hear, for to the one who has, more will be given, and from the one who has not, even what he thinks that he has will be taken away." God will remove the Judas-branches. Every superficial connection to Christ will be severed, one way or another. That is what 1 John 2:19 describes: "They went out from us, but they were not of us; for if they had been of us, they would have continued with us. But they went out, that it might become plain that they all are not of us."

Many, many religious people have only a superficial relationship with Christ. Some of them are deliberate, conscious hypocrites, and many others are self-deceived. But Jesus Himself said there are *many* who on judgment day will say to Him, "Lord, Lord, did we not prophesy in your name, and cast out demons in your name, and do many mighty works in your name?" (Matthew 7:22). He will declare to them, "I never knew you; depart from me, you workers of lawlessness" (v. 23). So be sure your connection to Christ is real and abiding. The apostle Paul admonishes us, "Examine yourselves, to see whether you are in the faith. Test yourselves. Or do you not realize this about yourselves, that Jesus Christ is in you?—unless indeed you fail to meet the test!" (2 Corinthians 13:5). We thus have a stern warning from Scripture to check our own lives and make sure our salvation is real. This is serious; a branch that does not bear fruit is taken away and burned.

Those who say the discarded branches are Christians have a problem: the branches are burned. If those branches are Christians, it would mean they have lost their salvation forever. But those fruitless branches are Judas-branches, false branches, people who associate themselves with Jesus and His Body and put on a facade of faith in Him—but it is *only* a facade. The heavenly Vinedresser will remove them.

THE FATHER PRUNES THE FRUITFUL BRANCHES

Although the fruitless branches are removed from the vine and burned, the Father tenderly cares for the fruit-bearing branches. Jesus told His disciples, "Every branch that does bear fruit he prunes, that it may bear more fruit" (John 15:2). The vinedresser prunes *all* the fruit-bearing branches so they will bear much fruit.

Kathairo is the original Greek word translated "prune." It's a word with a range of meanings, but the fundamental idea is that of cleansing. In farming, it referred to cleaning the husks off grain, or clearing the soil of weeds and stones before planting crops. In the metaphor of the vine, it refers to purging shoots from fruitful branches.

In first-century Palestine, vinedressers removed shoots in several ways. Sometimes the tip was pinched off to stop the growth. Larger branches were topped to prevent them from becoming too long and weak. Unwanted flower or grape clusters were thinned out.

Pruning is also necessary in our spiritual lives. The Father removes sins and the superfluous things that limit our fruitfulness. One of the best ways to cleanse us is to allow suffering and problems to come into our lives. Vinedressers often use a knife, which fits the metaphor. Sometimes when the heavenly Vinedresser puts us through the pruning process it hurts, and we may wonder if He knows what He's doing. He does. It may seem you are the only branch getting pruned while other branches need it more. But the Vinedresser knows exactly what He is doing, and He executes His work with impeccable skill.

Sufferings and trials can take many forms: sickness, hardships, loss of material possessions, persecution or slander from unbelievers. For some, it is the loss of a loved one or grief in a relationship. Whatever the method, spiritual pruning narrows our focus and strengthens the quality of our fruit.

During any time of pruning, we can be assured God cares about us and wants us to bear much fruit. He wants to free us from the shoots that drain our life and energy. He continues His care throughout our lives to keep us spiritually healthy and productive.

Knowing the Father's love and concern should change the way

we look at trials. He does not allow us to experience problems and struggles for no purpose. The problems He permits are designed to develop us so we can bear more fruit. "For the Lord disciplines the one he loves, and chastises every son whom he receives. . . . He disciplines us for our good, that we may share his holiness" (Hebrews 12:6, 10).

Do you look at trials and problems as pruning done by a loving Vinedresser? Or do you lapse into self-pity, fear, complaining, and brooding? Perhaps you feel God has good intentions but is not doing the pruning correctly. Maybe you ask, "God, why me? Why do I have to have problems when it seems like no one else does?"

If we remember that God is trying to make us more fruitful, we can look past the pruning process to the goal. It is thrilling to realize that God wants our lives to bear much fruit. Pruning can be painful. But the fruit—holiness—is well worth the process.

The Vinedresser's pruning knife is the Word of God. Jesus told the disciples. "Already you are clean because of the word that I have spoken to you" (John 15:3). The word here translated "clean" is the adjectival form of the verb He used in verse 2 to describe the pruning process. God's Word is the tool the Vinedresser uses to prune the sin out of our lives and stimulate fruitfulness.

He also uses affliction to make us more responsive to the Word. Most of us become more sensitive to the truth of Scripture when we are in trouble. When we have a particular problem, a verse of Scripture sometimes will seem to jump off the page. In adversity, the Word of God comes alive.

Charles Spurgeon said,

The Word is often the knife with which the great Husband-man prunes the vine; and, brothers and sisters, if we were more willing to feel the edge of the Word, and to let it cut away even something that may be very dear to us, we should not need so much pruning by affliction. It is because that first knife does not always produce the desired result that another sharp tool is used by which we are effectually pruned.[1]

The pruning process definitely helps us bear more fruit. If there is no fruit in your life—if there is no genuine connection to Jesus Christ—you are in danger of being removed and cast into the fire of hell. If there is fruit in your life, you can rejoice when God applies the pruning knife to make you more effective, and you can be glad, even in affliction, knowing that the Vinedresser's ultimate goal is that you bear much fruit.

---

1 Charles H. Spurgeon, *The Metropolitan Tabernacle Pulpit* (London: Passmore & Alabaster, 1899), 45:503.

Ten

———⟨✕✕⟩———

ABIDING
IN CHRIST

Scripture uses a number of metaphors to describe our relationship to Christ. He is the King and we are His subjects. He is the Master and we are His slaves. He is the Shepherd and we are His sheep. He is the head and we are His body. One of the finest metaphors is the one Christ Himself used in John 15, where He is the vine and we are the branches.

As we saw in the previous chapter, the vine-and-branches metaphor makes an ideal illustration of the Christian life. A branch grows through its connection with the vine, and we likewise grow spiritually only through our relationship with Christ. He is the source of our life and vitality, just as the vine is where a branch derives the nourishment and hydration that give it life. A branch is nothing apart from the vine, and we can do nothing apart from Christ. A branch draws strength from the vine, and we become strong through our connection with Christ.

As we have seen, in the metaphor of John 15, Christ is the vine and the Father is the vinedresser. The Father prunes the fruit-bearing branches to make them bear more fruit. He removes the fruitless branches, and they are burned. Through continual pruning, the fruitfulness of the vine is increased. The branches that abide in the vine—those who have a vital spiritual connection to Christ—are blessed; they grow and bear fruit, and the Father lovingly tends them.

As Jesus continues His teaching in John 15:7–11, He paints a beautiful picture of the Christian life and helps us understand and appreciate the blessings associated with abiding in Christ:

> If you abide in me, and my words abide in you, ask whatever you wish, and it will be done for you. By this my Father is glorified, that you bear much fruit and so prove to be my disciples. As the Father has loved me, so have I loved you. Abide in my love. If you keep my commandments, you will abide in my love, just as I have kept my Father's commandments and abide in his love. These things I have spoken to you, that my joy may be in you, and that your joy may be full.

That passage paints a beautiful picture of the Christian life. It magnifies six marvelous blessings associated with abiding in Christ: salvation, fruitfulness, answered prayer, abundant life, full joy, and security. Those are some of the key benefits of the believer's life in Christ, and each of them is worth a closer look.

SALVATION

As we noted in the previous chapter, the branches that abide in the true vine represent authentic believers. They are properly and permanently connected to the vine, drawing life and sustenance from the main trunk. When Jesus says in John 15:4, "Abide in me," that is meant as an encouragement to perseverance for the disciples. It also stands as a plea to any halfhearted and uncommitted readers of Scripture, urging them to repent of their hesitation and embrace Christ with settled, certain faith. It is in the same spirit as the warning passages scattered throughout the book of Hebrews, urging readers not to draw away from Christ before they have truly entered into His settled rest. They need to abide in Him in a deep and permanent way, not merely be hangers-on clinging superficially to the other branches.

If a person's relationship to Christ is genuine, he remains. The Word of God penetrates his life and stays with him, accomplishing its saving work in his heart. First John 2:24–25 says, "Let what you heard from the beginning abide in you. If what you heard from the beginning abides in you, then you too will abide in the Son and in the Father." Those who abide inherit eternal life.

That is not to say that it's possible to merit salvation by being steadfast. The opposite is true; God's saving work is what makes us truly steadfast. *He* "is able to keep you from stumbling and to present you blameless before the presence of his glory with great joy" (Jude v. 24). We are "guarded [by God's power] through faith for a salvation ready to be revealed in the last time" (1 Peter 1:5). Still, that steadfastness is the necessary evidence of authentic salvation. "We are not of those who shrink back and are destroyed, but of those who have faith and preserve their souls" (Hebrews 10:39).

Paul spoke of this divinely activated perseverance as an evidence of true salvation in Colossians 1:22–23: "He has now reconciled you in his body of flesh by his death, in order to present you holy and blameless and above reproach before him, if indeed you continue in the faith, stable and steadfast, not shifting from the hope of the gospel that you heard."

Hebrews 3:6 likewise says, "Christ is faithful over God's house as a son. And we are his house if indeed we hold fast our confidence and our boasting in our hope." By continuing in Christ we give evidence that we are really part of His household. Later, the same chapter says,

"For we have come to share in Christ, if indeed we hold our original confidence firm to the end" (v. 14). A true believer has a living and vital relationship with Jesus Christ that cannot give way to unbelief or apostasy.

Only the person who thus abides in the true vine can claim the promise of the constant presence of God. Jesus said, "Abide in me, and I in you" (John 15:4). As we saw in a previous chapter, that mutual indwelling speaks of a perfect union, guaranteeing Christ's permanent presence.

Many people come to church thinking that God is with them just because they sit in the pew. But being in a church doesn't mean the Lord is with you. He doesn't live inside a church building; He lives in His disciples. A person who sits among true disciples might be as far from Christ as the person in an isolated part of the world who has never heard the gospel—if he does not abide in the true vine.

Jesus says in verse 9, "As the Father has loved me, so have I loved you. Abide in my love." A real disciple doesn't come to Christ, receive His love, and then leave again; he remains. That is what Jesus is saying, whether He says "abide," "bear much fruit," or "abide in My love." They all mean, "Be sure you are a real believer."

A Christian can abide only by being firmly grounded in Jesus. If a branch is to abide, it cannot be even half an inch away—it must be fully connected. Those who are saved are those who are abiding, and those who are not abiding are not saved.

FRUITFULNESS

Those who truly abide will bear fruit. And no one can produce fruit independently of the vine. That is Jesus' point in verse 4: "Abide in me, and I in you. As the branch cannot bear fruit by itself, unless it abides in the vine, neither can you, unless you abide in me." The person who abides discovers that his soul is nourished with the truths of God as he stays in a close, living, energized relationship with Jesus Christ. The natural result of that is spiritual fruit.

Sometimes we think we can manufacture our own fruit. We become independent because we think we are strong or clever. Or sometimes we look at fruit we have borne in the past and think we can do it alone; we forget God worked through us to produce the fruit. But a branch can bear no fruit apart from the vine. Even strong branches can't bear fruit independently of the vine. The strongest branches, cut off from the vine, become as helpless as the weakest; the most beautiful are as helpless as the ugliest, and the best is as worthless as the worst.

Fruit bearing is not a matter of being strong or weak, good or bad, brave or cowardly, clever or foolish, experienced or inexperienced. Whatever your gifts, accomplishments, or virtues, they cannot produce fruit if you are detached from Jesus Christ.

Christians who think they are bearing fruit apart from the vine are only tying on artificial fruit. They run around grunting and groaning to produce fruit but accomplish nothing. Fruit is borne not by trying, but by abiding. To bear genuine fruit, you must take your place on the vine and get as close to Jesus as you can. Strip away all the things of the world. Put aside the sins that distract you and sap your energy. Put aside everything that robs you of a deep, personal, loving relationship with Jesus. Stay apart from sin and be in God's Word.

Having done all that, don't worry about bearing fruit. It is not your concern. The vine will merely use you to bear fruit. Get close to Jesus Christ, and His energy in you will bear fruit.

Some people find reading the Bible insipid and boring; they think sharing their faith is dull. Others find those things exciting. Invariably, the difference is that one is working on the deeds, and the other is concentrating on his relationship with Jesus Christ. Don't focus on the deeds; focus on your walk with Christ—the fruit will grow naturally out of your relationship.

Fruit is a frequent metaphor in Scripture. The main word for it is used approximately 100 times in the Old Testament and 70 times in the New Testament; it appears in 24 of the 27 New Testament books. It is mentioned often, yet it is also often misunderstood.

Fruit is not outward success. Many think that if a ministry is big and involves a lot of people, it is fruitful. But a church or Bible study group isn't successful just because it has many people—fleshly effort can produce big numbers. Some missionaries might minister to few people but bear much fruit.

Fruit bearing is not sensationalism. A person does not have a lot of fruit because he is enthusiastic or can make others enthusiastic about a church program. God produces real fruit in our lives when we abide.

The fruit of the Spirit is common to all of us, yet the Spirit uses each person differently. Fruit cannot be produced by simulating the genuine fruit another person has borne. It is tempting to see the fruit another person has produced and try to duplicate it. Instead of abiding, we try to manufacture the fruit we have seen in others, and we end up with wax fruit. God did not design us to fabricate artificial fruit. Our fruit is uniquely arranged, ordered, and designed by God, who loves variety.

Real fruit is, first of all, *Christlike character.* A believer who is like Christ is fruitful by definition. That is what Paul meant in Galatians 5:22–23, "The fruit of the Spirit is love, joy, peace, patience, kindness, goodness, faithfulness, gentleness, self-control." Those were all characteristics of Christ.

Christlike character is not produced by self-effort. It grows naturally out of a relationship with Him. We don't first try to be loving, and when we have become loving, try to be joyful, and so on. Instead, those qualities become part of our lives as we abide in Christ by staying close to Him.

Second, *thankful praise* to God is fruit. Hebrews 13:15 says, "Let us continually offer up a sacrifice of praise to God, that is, the fruit of lips that acknowledge his name." When you praise God and thank Him for who He is and what He has done, you offer Him fruit.

Help to those in need is a third kind of fruit to God. The Philippian church gave Paul a gift; in Philippians 4:17 he told them he was glad for their sake that they had met his need: "Not that I seek the gift, but I seek the fruit that increases to your credit." He saw the gift as an example of fruit in their lives. In the process of delivering a charitable gift from Macedonia and Achaia to the needy saints in Jerusalem, he told the church at Rome, "When therefore I have performed this, and have sealed to them this fruit, I will come by you into Spain" (Romans 15:28, KJV). Again he referred to a financial contribution for needy saints as "fruit." In both cases, their gifts revealed their love, so Paul spoke of it as spiritual fruit. A gift to someone in need is fruit if it is offered from a loving heart, in the divine energy of the indwelling Christ.

Purity in conduct is another kind of spiritual fruit. Paul wanted Christians to be holy in their behavior. He wrote in Colossians 1:10, "Walk in a manner worthy of the Lord, fully pleasing to him, bearing fruit in every good work and increasing in the knowledge of God."

Converts are another type of fruit. Many New Testament passages speak of converts as spiritual fruit. In 1 Corinthians 16:15, for example, Paul called the first converts in Achaia the "firstfruits of Achaia" (KJV). As you become closer to Him and more like Him, you will discover that sharing your faith is a natural outgrowth of abiding. You may not always see fruit immediately, but fruit will be borne, nevertheless.

When Jesus was traveling to Samaria, He met a woman getting

water. She told the people in her town about Jesus. As the people from the town came out to meet Him, He said to the disciples,

> Do you not say, "There are yet four months, then comes the harvest"? Look, I tell you, lift up your eyes, and see that the fields are white for harvest. Already the one who reaps is receiving wages and gathering fruit for eternal life, so that sower and reaper may rejoice together. For here the saying holds true, "One sows and another reaps." I sent you to reap that for which you did not labor. Others have labored, and you have entered into their labor. (John 4:35–38)

The disciples were reaping the results of other people's labor. Those people did not see all the result of their labor, but their efforts still bore fruit.

William Carey spent seven years in India before he saw one convert. Some people think those were wasted years. But almost every convert in India to this day is fruit on his branch, because he translated the whole New Testament into many different Indian dialects. He was not the one to reap directly what he had sown, but his life's legacy bore much fruit.

One of the most fulfilling experiences in life is to bear fruit for God. If it isn't happening in your life, the reason is simple—you are not abiding in the vine.

ANSWERED PRAYER

God gives an incredible promise to those who abide: "If you abide in me, and my words abide in you, ask whatever you wish, and it will be done for you" (John 15:7). Notice that there are two conditions to that promise. First, we must abide. "Abide," as we have seen, speaks of a permanent, secure connection to Christ. It refers to salvation. This promise is only for real believers.

Of course, in His sovereign wisdom, God sometimes answers the prayers of a non-Christian, but He does not obligate Himself to do so. If He does, it is His sovereign choice and for His purpose; He does not have to. The promise of answered prayer is reserved only for those who abide in the true Vine.

Still, many who are true branches do not always get the answers they are looking for when they pray. It may be because they are not meeting Jesus' second condition, which is, "If . . . my words abide in you." That's not speaking only about the very words Christ Himself spoke. Some people misuse red-letter Bibles because they regard the words of Jesus as more inspired or more important than the words of other writers of Scripture. But the words of Paul, Peter, John, and Jude are just as important. The Lord Jesus Christ has spoken through all of Scripture; it is *all* His message to us. Therefore, when He says, "If . . . my words abide in you," He means we must have such high regard for all of Scripture that we let it abide in us, that we hide it in our hearts, and that we commit ourselves to knowing and obeying it.

To meet the first condition, a person must be a Christian. To meet the second condition, he must study Scripture in order to govern his life by what Christ has revealed.

The same principle is implied in John 14:14, "If you ask me anything in my name, I will do it." When we studied that text in chapter 5, we made the point that praying in Jesus' name is not merely adding magic words to the end of a prayer. It means praying for that which is consistent with the words and will of Christ. The Christian who is abiding in Christ and controlled by His Word is not going to ask anything against God's will, because he wants what God wants. That person is guaranteed an answer to his prayer.

Our prayers often go unanswered because we pray selfishly. James 4:3 says, "You ask and do not receive, because you ask wrongly, to spend it on your passions."

Our prayers will be answered if we follow Paul's example in 2 Corinthians 10:5, "We destroy arguments and every lofty opinion raised against the knowledge of God, and take every thought captive to obey Christ." We must rid our minds of everything that contradicts God's truth or violates His will. When we *think* according to the will of God, we *pray* accordingly—and such prayers are always answered.

There is so little power in the prayers of the church today because we are not fully abiding and seeking His mind. Instead of bringing our minds into obedience to Christ and asking according to His will, we ask selfishly, so our prayers go unanswered. If we cultivated an intimate love relationship with Christ, we would desire what He desires; and we would ask and receive.

The psalmist said, "Delight yourself in the Lord, and he will give you the desires of your heart" (Psalm 37:4). That means that when you delight completely in the Lord, He implants the right desires in your heart—then fulfills them. His desires become yours. What a blessing it is to know that God will answer every prayer we bring to Him!

ABUNDANT LIFE

Abiding in Christ is the source of the abundant life Jesus spoke of in John 10:10. Those who abide fulfill the magnificent purpose of life, which is to give God the glory He deserves. Jesus said in John 15:8, "By this my Father is glorified, that you bear much fruit and so prove to be my disciples." When a Christian abides, God can work through him to produce much fruit. Since God produces the fruit, He is the One glorified.

Paul recognized the source of fruit in his life. He said in Romans 15:18, "I will not venture to speak of anything except what Christ has accomplished through me." He did not tell people how good he was at preaching or evangelism. He recognized that everything worthwhile in his life came from God.

In Galatians 2:20 he said, "I have been crucified with Christ. It is no longer I who live, but Christ who lives in me. And the life I now live in the flesh I live by faith in the Son of God, who loved me and gave himself for me." He knew God was the source of everything praiseworthy in him, so God alone deserved all the glory.

Peter had the same idea in mind when he said in 1 Peter 2:12, "Keep your conduct among the Gentiles honorable, so that when they speak against you as evildoers, they may see your good deeds and glorify God."

So this is the logical progression: the one who abides bears fruit; God is glorified in the fruit because He is the One who deserves credit for it; the purpose of life is fulfilled because God is glorified; and thus the one who abides and glorifies God experiences abundant life.

FULL JOY

One of the chief elements of the abundant life is fullness of joy, which is an outgrowth of abiding in the true Vine. Jesus says in John 15:11, "These things I have spoken to you, that my joy may be in you, and that your joy may be full."

God wants us to be consumed with joy, but few Christians are. Churches have many people who are bitter, discontented, and complaining. Some people think the Christian life is monastic deprivation and drudgery—a bitter religious pill. But God has designed it for our joy. It is when we violate God's design that we lose our joy. If we abide fully, we will have full joy.

When David sinned, he no longer sensed the presence of God. He cried out in Psalm 51:12, "Restore to me the joy of your salvation." He had allowed sin to hinder the pure abiding relationship. He did not lose his salvation, but he lost the *joy* of his salvation.

That joy returned when he confessed his sin and accepted the consequences of it. His guilt was removed; he returned to a pure, unhindered, abiding relationship; and his joy was made full again.

To make a point that is very similar to what we learned in chapter 7, the joy of abiding in the true Vine is unaffected by external circumstances, persecution, or the disappointments of life. We can experience the same joy Jesus had. And His joy flows through those who abide in Him.

SECURITY

Abiding in the true Vine brings the deepest kind of security. Romans 8:1 says, "There is therefore now no condemnation for those who are in Christ Jesus." Those who are in Him cannot be removed, they cannot be cut off, and they need not fear judgment. There is no suggestion here that those who now abide might later cease to do so. Their position is secure.

On the other hand, those who do not abide will be judged. Jesus says in John 15:6, "If anyone does not abide in me he is thrown away like a branch and withers; and the branches are gathered, thrown into the fire, and burned." Again: those are the Judas-branches—false disciples. Since they have no living connection to Jesus Christ, they are cast out.

The true believer could never be thrown away. Jesus promises in John 6:37, "All that the Father gives me will come to me, and whoever comes to me I will never cast out." If a person is cast forth, it is because he was never a real disciple.

The branches that are cast off are gathered and burned. They burn forever and ever in flames that can never be quenched. It is a tragic and vivid picture of God's judgment. The parable of the wheat and tares tells us that the angels of God gather those destined for judgment. Jesus says in Matthew 13:41–42, "The Son of Man will send his angels, and they will gather out of his kingdom all causes of sin and all law-breakers, and throw them into the fiery furnace. In that place there will be weeping and gnashing of teeth."

There will be a day when God sends His angels to gather from around the world all the Judas-branches who have no connection to Christ. He will cast them into eternal hell. It is tragic when a person appears to be a genuine branch but ends up in hell.

William Pope was a member of the Methodist Church in England for most of his life. He made a pretense of knowing Christ and served in many capacities. His wife died a genuine believer.

Soon, however, he began to drift from Christ. He had companions who believed in the redemption of demons. He began going with them to the public house of prostitution. In time, he became a drunkard. He admired Thomas Paine and would assemble with his friends on Sundays when they would confirm each other in their infidelity. They amused themselves by throwing the Bible on the floor and kicking it around.

Then he contracted tuberculosis. Someone visited him and told him of the great Redeemer. He said Pope could be saved from the punishment of his sins.

But Pope replied, "I have no contrition; I cannot repent. God will damn me! I know the day of grace is lost. God has said to such as me, 'I will laugh at your calamity, and mock when your fear cometh.' I have denied him; my heart is hardened."

Then he cried, "Oh, the hell, the pain I feel! I have chosen my way. I have done the horrible damnable deed; I have crucified the Son of God afresh; I have counted the blood of the covenant an unholy thing! Oh that wicked and horrible thing of blaspheming the Holy Spirit, which I know that I have committed; I want nothing but hell! Come, oh devil and take me!"[1]

Pope had spent most of his life in the church, but his end was infinitely worse than his beginning. Every man has the same choice. You can abide in the Vine and receive all of God's blessings, or you can be burned.

It doesn't seem like a difficult choice, does it? Yet millions of people resist God's gift of salvation, preferring the superficial relationship of the false branch. Perhaps you know people like that—or perhaps you are like that yourself. If so, Jesus' plea to you is a loving invitation: "Abide in Me, and I in you."

---

1 John Myers, *Voices from the Edge of Eternity* (Old Tappan, NJ: Spire, 1972). 147–49.

Eleven

⟵—◇◇◇—⟶

THE FRIENDS
OF JESUS

Ancient oriental kings often relied on a select group of advisers, special friends of the monarch, who functioned much like the cabinet of a modern American president. But those were far more than mere political consultants—they were his intimate friends. They protected and cared for him and were given immediate access to him. They could even enter his bedchamber. He valued their advice more than that of generals, statesmen, or rulers of other nations. No one was closer to the king.

The royal advisers' role was one that transcended the king-subject or master-disciple relationship. It was a position of intimate friendship, a bond of love and trust that superseded formality, protocol, or any external threat.

Jesus cultivated that kind of relationship with His disciples, and in His final words to them on the night before He died, He repeatedly affirmed that He valued the intimacy they shared. The time had come that He must leave them, but He wanted them to be sure of their status as His friends.

This is my commandment, that you love one another as I have loved you. Greater love has no one than this, that someone lay down his life for his friends. You are my friends if you do what I command you. No longer do I call you servants, for the servant does not know what his master is doing; but I have called you friends, for all that I have heard from my Father I have made known to you. You did not choose me, but I chose you and appointed you that you should go and bear fruit and that your fruit should abide, so that whatever you ask the Father in my name, he may give it to you. (John 15:12–16)

The Greek word for "slave" or "servant" is *doulos*. Obviously, being a slave in any context is not a position of high rank. But in Jewish culture the idea of being *God's* servant carried no stigma or shame whatsoever. Four verses in the Old Testament—1 Chronicles 6:49; 2 Chronicles 24:9; Nehemiah 10:29; and Daniel 9:11—refer to "Moses the servant of God." God Himself frequently referred to Moses as "my servant." If Moses bore that title, it was no rank of disgrace.

To be known as the *friend* of God, however, was an unimaginably high honor. Abraham is the only one in the Old Testament upon whom God conferred the title. Everyone familiar with the Jewish Scriptures would have been aware of the uniqueness of Abraham's place as God's friend. So Jesus' words to the eleven remaining disciples must have left them breathless.

Because of their love and devotion to Christ, the disciples would no doubt have been quite happy to be known as Jesus' servants. As we saw in chapter 1, they loved status and frequently argued over who was the greatest. They weren't always keen to serve one another. But they gladly served *Christ*. In effect, when they chose to follow Him and become disciples, they assumed the role of His servants. There was no dishonor or disgrace whatsoever in that standing.

All of them had craved a close friendship of deep affection with Him—that's no doubt one of the reasons they contended among themselves about which one would sit closest to Him in the kingdom. (Surely that jockeying for position wasn't motivated *only* by a concern for personal status.) Now He reassured all of them that He too desired that same kind of intimacy with them, and He listed a number of the characteristics essential to an intimate relationship with Him.

OBEDIENCE

The first characteristic is obedience, which sums up the essence of friendship with Christ. Actually, because He is rightfully Lord of all, obedience is an absolute condition for a friendly relationship with Him. In verse 10, Jesus says. "If you keep my commandments, you will abide in my love, just as I have kept my Father's commandments and abide in his love." Then in verse 14 He adds, "You are my friends if you do what I command you." That is not to say that friendship with Him is either earned or attained by any amount of human effort, but rather that obedience is an identifying mark of all true friends of Jesus. In fact, those who obey God share intimacy with Jesus as members of the same family. Jesus had explained before that obedience is characteristic of all those in His spiritual family:

His mother and his brothers came, and standing outside they sent to him and called him. And a crowd was sitting around him, and they said to him, "Your mother and your brothers are outside, seeking you."

And he answered them, "Who are my mother and my brothers?" And looking about at those who sat around him, he said, "Here are my mother and my brothers! For whoever does the will of God, he is my brother and sister and mother." (Mark 3:31–35)

Scripture also speaks of the relationship of believers with Jesus as that of sheep who follow their Shepherd. Jesus says in John 10:27, "My sheep hear my voice, and I know them, and they follow me." Again, intimacy depends on willing obedience. In every metaphor Jesus ever used to describe His relationship with His disciples, obedience was an essential condition. In John 8:31 He says, "If you abide in my word, you are truly my disciples." Intimacy with Jesus Christ is always built on a foundation of obedience, whether it is the intimacy of a sheep and a shepherd, a teacher and a disciple, family members, or simply friends.

First John 3:9–10 refers to that identifying mark of the family of God: "No one born of God makes a practice of sinning, for God's seed abides in him, and he cannot keep on sinning because he has been born of God. By this it is evident who are the children of God, and who are the children of the devil: whoever does not practice righteousness is not of God."

Again, a person does not *become* a child of God through obedience—that would make salvation depend on good works. Rather, obedience is proof that a person is intimately connected with Jesus Christ through faith. It does not qualify someone to be a child of God. It only demonstrates that he is one.

LOVE FOR EACH OTHER

A second characteristic of friendship with Jesus is love for fellow believers: "This is my commandment, that you love one another as I have loved you. Greater love has no one than this, that someone lay down his life for his friends" (John 15:12–13). The friends of Jesus have a deep, sincere, and abiding love for other Christians.

Love is a great source of personal fulfillment, and the world is hungry for it. But friends of Jesus are the only ones who can truly experience the love the world is seeking. Unbelievers know nothing of the love believers can share, because it comes from a source they cannot know. "We love because he first loved us" (1 John 4:19). Love is a fruit of the Spirit (Galatians 5:22). Romans 5:5 says, "God's love has been poured into our hearts through the Holy Spirit who has been given to us." The Christian overflows with the love of God: he lives in it, and it lives in him.

You cannot be a true believer without having love for other believers: "Whoever says he is in the light and hates his brother is still in darkness. Whoever loves his brother abides in the light, and in him there is no cause for stumbling. But whoever hates his brother is in the darkness and walks in the darkness, and does not know where he is going, because the darkness has blinded his eyes" (1 John 2:9–11). John further explains: "Everyone who believes that Jesus is the Christ has been born of God, and everyone who loves the Father loves whoever has been born of him" (5:1).

That is not to say that if we ever fail to love another Christian to the fullest, it proves we are not true believers. A Christian may sometimes fail to love a brother or sister in Christ the way he should. But John is not explaining exceptions to the rule—he is describing the general pattern believers follow.

It is natural for a true friend of Jesus to love other friends of Jesus. Paul writes, "Now concerning brotherly love you have no need for anyone to write to you, for you yourselves have been taught by God to love one another" (1 Thessalonians 4:9). To be unloving to another

Christian, a Christian has to violate his new nature in Christ, resist the love that is natural to his new nature, and choose sin instead.

Jesus wants us to love just as He loves. He showed His deep desire when He said, "Love one another *as I have loved you.* Greater love has no one than this, that someone lay down his life for his friends" (John 15:12–13, emphasis added). Of course our love cannot be on the same scale as His—He died for the sins of the world. But we can love the way He loves. We can be sacrificial and selfless. We can go beyond an external love and love with a love that is total and self-giving.

No fellow believer is a mere acquaintance. Whoever he or she is, we share a common spiritual heritage. We should see them as Christ sees them. Love should move us to give our wealth, to bear burdens, to feel what another feels, and to hurt where another hurts. We should be willing to comfort, to sacrifice, to instruct, and to support—just the way Christ would.

The quality of our love is our testimony for Christ. Because only Christians have God's love in their lives, the world should see the greatest love in Christians. Jesus says in John 13:35, "By this all people will know that you are my disciples, if you have love for one another." The depth of sacrifice one is willing to make reveals the intensity of love. Giving up one's life has always been recognized as the supreme expression of love. Jesus was about to show He had that kind of love for His disciples. He told them, "Greater love has no one than this" (John 15:13).

Too many who claim to know Christ are far from sacrificing their lives—they will not even give up a few minutes of time. Money is needed for ministries around the world, but the needs go unfulfilled because too many Christians do not give sacrificially. Many who say they love the Lord will not even tell someone about Him, nor will they use their spiritual gifts to help another believer grow.

Christians fall far short of dying for others. Some have not even learned how to *live* for others. True love requires total sacrifice. When we love the way Christ did, the world will listen to our message. It is pointless to ask unbelievers to trust Christ when they cannot see His love operating in us.

Jesus sacrificed to the utmost, even for the unlovable. Paul says in Romans 5:7–8, "For one will scarcely die for a righteous person— though perhaps for a good person one would dare even to die—but God shows his love for us in that while we were still sinners, Christ died for us."

How do you know Christ loves you? Because He laid down His life. First John 3:16 says this: "By this we know love, that he laid down his life for us, and we ought to lay down our lives for the brothers."

When my eldest son, Matt, was very young, he would often say to me, "I love you, Dad." I would ask him, "How much do you love me?" He would answer, "I love you big much." I would ask, "How much is big much?" He would jump into my lap, put his arms around my neck, squeeze as tight as he could, and say, "That's big much."

If we could ask God, "How much do you love me?" I believe He would answer by pointing to a rocky hillside outside Jerusalem and saying, "Do you see the cross in the middle? My Son is on it. I love you that much."

Are you ready to lay down your life for another? Do you love sacrificially? Are you caring for the needs of others? Needs are all around you. Some people need to be taught; some need reproof; others need restoration. There are physical needs, and many people who need prayer.

We say we love people, but do we meet their needs?

Love is always practical. The apostle John wrote, "If anyone has the world's goods and sees his brother in need, yet closes his heart against him, how does God's love abide in him?" (1 John 3:17). John then encourages the children of God to prove their love in an active way: "Little children, let us not love in word or talk but in deed and in truth" (v. 18). The true friend of Jesus meets the needs of others.

A KNOWLEDGE OF DIVINE TRUTH

In Jesus' day, slaves and their masters were rarely friends. They were not necessarily enemies. They simply did not cultivate the kind of relationship friends would have. A slave was told only what he should do, never why he should do it. He never knew his master's plans, goals, or feelings. He was merely a functionary who did what he was told—a living tool rarely included in the sharing of rewards. It was different between Jesus and His disciples. He told them, "No longer do I call you servants, for the servant does not know what his master is doing; but I have called you friends, for all that I have heard from my Father I have made known to you" (John 15:15).

Surrender to Jesus Christ is never blind obedience. He shares with His friends everything He has received from the Father. They share His heart for His work because they know the whole plan from beginning to end. It is the truest kind of friendship. If we are His friends, we want what He wants, and we do His will because it is our heart's desire.

Jesus promised the disciples special insight, "If you abide in my word, you are truly my disciples, and you will know the truth, and the truth will set you free" (John 8:31–32). Everything the Father told Him, He passed on to them. Consider His prayer to the Father: "I have manifested your name to the people whom you gave me out of the world. Yours they were, and you gave them to me, and they have kept your word. Now they know that everything that you have given me is from you. For I have given them the words that you gave me, and they have received them and have come to know in truth that I came from you; and they have believed that you sent me" (John 17:6–8).

Through His parables Jesus taught the disciples the mysteries of God's plan. Matthew writes, "The disciples came and said to him, 'Why do you speak to them in parables?' And he answered them, 'To you it has been given to know the secrets of the kingdom of heaven, but to them it has not been given'" (Matthew 13:10–11).

As a result, the disciples had special knowledge others sought but never found. Jesus told them, "Blessed are the eyes that see what you see! For I tell you that many prophets and kings desired to see what you see, and did not see it, and to hear what you hear, and did not hear it" (Luke 10:23–24).

So spiritual knowledge passed from the Father through Jesus to the apostles. The apostles passed it to us through the Scriptures. Paul writes in Romans 16:25–26 of "the mystery that was kept secret for long ages but has now been disclosed and through the prophetic writings has been made known to all nations, according to the command of the eternal God, to bring about the obedience of faith."

Spiritual understanding sets Christians apart. The things of God are spiritually discerned, and the unredeemed mind cannot understand them (1 Corinthians 2:12–16). A philosopher or scientist who seeks spiritual truth apart from the Word of God and the Spirit of God knows little compared to the simplest Christian.

Jesus did not expect His disciples to follow Him without knowing where He was leading; they were not being enslaved to a mechanical kind of obedience. They were His friends, and He revealed to them the truth He could not share with those not intimate with Him.

A DIVINE APPOINTMENT

Another characteristic of Jesus' friends is that they have been chosen by God and appointed to a position of service. Friendships are usually formed when two people choose to befriend each other. But a friendship with Jesus Christ is formed at His initiative. Jesus chose twelve men to be His disciples—they did not simply volunteer. Luke 6:13 records, "when day came, he called his disciples and chose from them twelve, whom he named apostles."

Jesus reminded them, "You did not choose me, but I chose you and appointed you" (John 15:16). He further told them, "I chose you out of the world" (v. 19). The Greek word for "appointed" is *tithemi,* a word with a range of meanings, including "ordain," "kneel," and "prostrate." It signifies a stately appointment—a formal ordination.

Paul uses the same word in 1 Corinthians 12:28, where he says, "God has *appointed* in the church first apostles, second prophets, third teachers . . . " (emphasis added). He uses it again in 2 Timothy 1:11, where he refers to the gospel as the message "for which I was *appointed* a preacher and apostle and teacher" (emphasis added).

In both places, Paul is referring to being chosen to specific service. In fact, throughout Scripture, wherever the doctrine of God's sovereign choice—*election*—is discussed, the context always goes beyond salvation. That's because whenever God elects someone to salvation, He also ordains him or her to special service. Therefore, the friends of Jesus are not chosen just for salvation; they are chosen to do something: "I chose you and appointed you that you should go and bear fruit and that your fruit should abide" (John 15:16). We have not been chosen to stand and watch the world go by.

I was once speaking at a conference of university students and met a young man who had dropped out of seminary. When I asked him what he was doing in the Lord's service, he said he was involved in a Bible study group he hoped would grow into a church. "We just have a little fellowship and praise God together," he said, with emphasis. I asked who taught them. He replied, "Nobody teaches us; we just share. No one ever teaches." I then asked, "What do you feel is your purpose?" "Well," he said, "we just praise the Lord a lot."

I asked if they were involved in evangelism. "No," he said. "We've been in existence two and a half years, and we've never done any kind of outreach or publicity. We don't feel we are called to that. We are still an infant church with a few young Christians. So evangelism isn't really a priority yet."

He seemed to have the idea they were called to sit with each other and sing. It is good to praise God and fellowship, but we are also called to *go*. The Bible does not command those who are in the world to come to church. It commands those in the church to "Go out to the highways and hedges and compel people to come in" (Luke 14:23). Jesus' last commission to His followers was, "Go into all the world and proclaim the gospel to the whole creation" (Mark 16:15). He promised the disciples, "You will receive power when the Holy Spirit has come upon you, and you will be my witnesses in Jerusalem and in all Judea and Samaria, and to the end of the earth" (Acts 1:8).

Jesus chose a group of men out of the world of darkness. He saved them, loved them, and trained them. He called them His friends. Then He sent them back into the world to tell everyone about Him.

It is our high calling and privilege to glorify the name of Christ in the world. We are called and ordained to let God work His perfect will through us. Thus, life has purpose for the Christian. When we communicate the gospel and a person responds by receiving Christ, we have witnessed a Spirit-energized transformation that will last for eternity. It is so different from the unbeliever, whose life dwindles away without meaning, day after day with no eternal results. The Christian's life makes ripples throughout eternity, because our fruit remains. Revelation 14:13 says of the dead in Christ, "They may rest from their labors, for their deeds follow them!"

John 15:16 concludes with a promise from Jesus: "Whatever you ask the Father in my name, he [will] give it to you." As we have seen before, that means we must ask the Father for the things Jesus would want. We cannot use prayer as a way to satisfy our lusts. We must be unselfish if we are to ask in His name. Praying in His name means asking according to God's will. If we do that, the answer is guaranteed.

We who have trusted in His name are all friends of Jesus Christ. We are not like subjects who crowd the streets, hoping to catch a glimpse of the king as he passes by. We have the right to enter His presence anytime. We are the people closest to our King. It is thrilling to know we are the personal friends of the Creator and King of the universe.

All people are either friends of Jesus Christ or friends of the world. Friendship with the world is hostility toward God. Friendship with Jesus Christ is intimacy with God. It is fellowship with the Trinity. It is unspeakable joy and full of glory. Such blessings, if they are not already yours, can belong to you today if you will repent of your sins, renounce the world, and respond to Christ's call to be your Lord and Savior—and your friend.

Twelve

———————⊰✕⊱———————

HATED WITHOUT
A CAUSE

In 1971, when I had been in pastoral ministry less than three years, a young man from the college department in our church was physically attacked while he was handing out tracts in a Southern California park. He was a gentle soul, who never had a bad thing to say about anyone and wasn't the least bit contentious, but he loved to share the good news of Jesus Christ, even with strangers on the street. Someone was evidently angered by his mere presence and beat him into unconsciousness. It was a brutal beating, but he recovered, and soon he was back on the streets, telling people about Christ. He had not lost any of his zeal for the Lord.

A few weeks later this same young man was witnessing for Christ at Seventh and Broadway in downtown Los Angeles. It was 4:40 in the afternoon, the height of rush hour and the end of the business day. He was talking with passersby, handing out gospel tracts, when he was attacked again, this time with a hard blow to the head from behind. The back of his skull was fractured in four places. At the hospital, doctors drilled three holes in his skull to relieve the pressure, but they were unsuccessful. Three days later he died. He was committed to proclaiming Jesus Christ to a Christ-hating world, and he paid for it with his life.

That incident helped change my perspective on the cost of serving Christ in a hostile world. It is too easy to have a casual attitude toward persecution when we read about how it has affected believers in ancient times or in other parts of the world. But when such murderous hostility strikes so close to home, it is a much more sobering experience.

When Luke recorded Jesus' commission in Acts 1:8 that His disciples were to be His "witnesses," he used the Greek word *martus,* from which we get the English word *martyr.* Although it originally meant "witness," so many in the early church who witnessed for Christ were killed that the word came to refer primarily to a person who died for his testimony for Christ.

Jesus wanted the disciples to know they would meet hostility when they witnessed for Him. But on the night before He died, His purpose was primarily to comfort and reassure them. The bulk of His discourse that night consisted of words of comfort and encouragement. He saved until last what He had to say about the persecution they would face after He left.

Jesus told the disciples of His love (John 13), and He gave them tremendous promises (John 14). He promised He was going to prepare a place for them and that He would return to take them there (vv. 2–3). He told them that they would do greater works than He had done (v. 12). He said they could ask anything in His name and He would do it (v. 13). He promised that the Holy Spirit would live in them and be their Helper (v. 16). He reassured them they would be intensely loved by Him and by the Father (v. 23). He said the disciples would possess divine life and knowledge (v 26). And He promised to give His peace (v. 27).

Next Jesus told the disciples they would bear fruit for God (John 15:5). He promised that they would abide and be closely connected to Him (v. 10); that they would have His joy (v. 11); and that His life would flow through them. Finally, He called them His friends (v. 14).

But in addition to all those promises, Christ needed to warn His closest friends. They needed to know that, in spite of the wonderful divine promises that would be fulfilled in their experience, life would not be completely blissful. Ministry would not be easy in a rebellious, Christ-hating world. The world was going to treat them the same way it treated Him. They were going to be despised and persecuted—even killed.

Verse 17 is Jesus' transition from describing His love for the disciples to describing the world's hatred: "These things I command you, so that you will love one another." The Greek verb indicates a continuous action: "Keep on loving each other," He is saying. "Devote yourselves to one another and sacrifice for one another. Love each other the way I loved you." That's a simple summary of everything He had been saying all evening.

Now the tone and topic change:

> If the world hates you, know that it has hated me before it hated you. If you were of the world, the world would love you as its own; but because you are not of the world, but I chose you out of the world, therefore the world hates you. Remember the word that I said to you: "A servant is not greater than his master." If they persecuted me, they will also persecute you. If they kept my word, they will also keep yours. But all these things they will do to you on account of my name, because they do not know him who sent me. If I had not come and spoken to them, they would not have been guilty of sin, but

195

now they have no excuse for their sin. Whoever hates me hates my Father also. If I had not done among them the works that no one else did, they would not be guilty of sin, but now they have seen and hated both me and my Father. But the word that is written in their Law must be fulfilled: "They hated me without a cause." (John 15:17–25)

One reason their love for each other was so important was that the world would know nothing but hatred for them. Love for each other was the only love they would ever know. In a hostile world, they desperately needed love from each other.

History shows that the apostles were indeed hated. Just as Jesus predicted, practically all of them paid with their lives for their testimony about Jesus. Of the twelve, James was martyred first. Andrew persisted in preaching and was tied to a cross and crucified. Peter, too, was crucified—and the story comes down to us from the early church that Peter was crucified upside down because he did not consider himself worthy of the same death as his Savior. According to Christian tradition, all of them were martyred except John, who was sent into exile on Patmos.[1]

All Christ's followers in the first three centuries lived under the threat of persecution. The Roman government attacked the church in several waves. The emperor Nero beheaded the apostle Paul. Roman officials tended to regard Christians as disloyal citizens and a threat to the unity of the empire, because of their confession that Jesus is Lord of all. Rome was concerned about unity because the empire stretched from the Euphrates River to England and from Germany to North Africa. It included a wide variety of peoples and cultures. Such

---

1 For more about the twelve and what became of them, see John MacArthur, *Twelve Ordinary Men* (Nashville: Nelson, 2002).

a multicultural empire could easily become divided. From the time of Caesar Augustus on, Rome viewed emperor worship as a way to bond the different peoples of the vast empire. All Roman citizens were therefore required to worship Caesar. Once a year, they had to demonstrate their allegiance by burning a pinch of incense to acknowledge the deity of Caesar. Then they were required to shout, "Caesar is Lord!" As long as they worshiped the emperor, citizens could also worship any other god they wished.

But Christians would call no man lord. The government therefore considered them disloyal, and the rest of society marginalized them, too. They were sometimes disparagingly referred to as "atheists" because of their refusal to acknowledge the official god of Rome. Insults, deliberate defamation, and accusations stemming from ignorance added to believers' woes. They were accused of cannibalism because they talked about eating the flesh and drinking the blood of Christ at their communion services. Some accused the Christians of immorality, thinking the Christian "love feast" was some kind of orgy. Because Christians expected the second coming of their King, some thought they were planning a rebellion. They were suspected of arson because they said God was going to bring fire on judgment day. (They were actually blamed for the burning of Rome in the first century.)

Although the flavor and intensity of the world's persecution may vary from generation to generation, hostility toward Christianity has been a constant throughout church history. Indeed, anti-Christian persecution is a surprisingly widespread—and growing— problem in the world today, not only in the parts of the world that are dominated by other religions, but also in countries where religious liberty was once celebrated. In America, for example, secularists have waged a daunting campaign for nearly five decades to drive the church out of the public square. Christian values and biblical convictions are increasingly under attack from the government, the media, and the entertainment industry. Most persecution in our culture today consists chiefly of scorn, insults, and legal threats. But with the current drift of public opinion, it may not be long before the church in the West begins to face persecution on a scale comparable to what the early church suffered.

The world's hostility is not something we can evade without compromising. Jesus gives three main reasons suffering and persecution are unavoidable for faithful disciples.

CHRIST'S FOLLOWERS ARE NOT OF THE WORLD

First of all, Jesus' disciples are rejected by the world because they are no longer a part of the world's system. Jesus told the apostles, "If you were of the world, the world would love you as its own; but because you are not of the world, but I chose you out of the world, therefore the world hates you" (John 15:19). Authentic believers in Christ simply cannot fit into the world's system. We are supposed to be different. We have different values, a different Lord, and a completely different agenda.

"World" is the English translation of *kosmos,* a common word in Greek. It appears often in John's writings, and its meaning is always determined by the context. Here it refers to an evil system consisting of the twisted values, unrighteous ambitions, and hostile powers that dominate this earthly realm under the influence of the Devil. It includes people, institutions, laws, customs, power structures, and even the cultural milieu—wherever profane or materialistic values are embraced.

In short, the *kosmos* is an expression of satanic wickedness and human depravity. It is set against Christ, His people, and His kingdom. Satan and his evil minions are in control of it.

This evil world system is incapable of authentic, godly love. When Jesus said the world loves its own, His point was not that worldlings genuinely love each other. "Its own" is not a masculine plural, which would indicate a love directed toward other people. The word in the Greek text is neuter plural, meaning that the people caught up in the world love their own *things*. A worldly individual loves himself and his own things. He loves others only if it is to his advantage. The world's love is always selfish, superficial, and interested primarily in whatever benefits can be gained for oneself. That's why people talk about falling in and out of love. Their affections are determined by whatever offers them some kind of pleasure or advantage at the moment.

The *kosmos* is dead set against those who love and follow Jesus—those who declare their faith in Him and show it by their words and deeds. The world does not persecute those who are part of its system. Jesus said to His earthly brothers, who did not follow Him until after the resurrection, "The world cannot hate you, but it hates me because I testify about it that its works are evil" (John 7:7).

People living in the world who do not know Jesus Christ are part of a system that is anti-God, anti-Christ, and satanic. That system militates against God and His principles. It is opposed to all that is good, godly, and Christlike. I am always amazed at the way some Christians seem to believe the world can easily be persuaded to admire Jesus if we try to portray Him as a stylish superstar to be idolized. That failed (and still failing) strategy is one of the major reasons persecution is on the rise. In any contest for the world's affections, the truth will always be marginalized. "The light has come into the world, and people loved the darkness rather than the light because their works were evil" (John 3:19). No unbeliever will ever truly embrace Christ apart from the Holy Spirit's convicting and regenerating work. The church's duty is to preach the Word of God and proclaim the gospel—even in the face of the world's hostility.

It is true that much of the world is religious, but religion is not the same as righteousness. Some false religions display a superficial tolerance toward the things of God. Still, they are tools of Satan in his war against the truth. They disguise themselves with the appearance of godliness, but they deny the true power of God (2 Timothy 3:5). They reveal their real nature by suppressing the truth. Throughout history, false religion has been the most aggressive opponent of the true church.

Ultimately, persecution is inevitable for righteous people living in the world. Paul warned Timothy, "Indeed, all who desire to live a godly life in Christ Jesus will be persecuted, while evil people and impostors will go on from bad to worse, deceiving and being deceived" (2 Timothy 3:12–13). Abuse from the world is an inescapable fact of godly living.

People who profess to be Christians but never personally experience any antagonism from the world need to examine themselves. Perhaps they haven't faithfully declared their faith, so that it is not obvious to their non-Christian neighbors what they believe. Perhaps they are not genuine Christians at all. A true believer should stand out in the eyes of the world because he has been made holy through identification with Jesus Christ. He lives by markedly different values. He pursues righteousness and does not derive his identity from the world system. He doesn't love the same things worldly people love. A genuine Christian represents God and Christ, and that is why Satan uses the world's system to attack him. That is why Jesus prayed for the Father's protection of His followers: "I do not ask that you take them out of the world, but that you keep them from the evil one" (John 17:15).

Our lives are to be a rebuke to the sinful world. Ephesians 5:11 says, "Take no part in the unfruitful works of darkness, but instead expose them." One of the reasons we may not feel as much hatred from the world as Jesus said we would is that our lives are not really a rebuke to the world's conscience. To live for Christ in a hostile and perverted world, we must be blameless. Paul, writing to the Philippian church, cautioned them to avoid sin, "that you may be blameless and innocent, children of God without blemish in the midst of a crooked and twisted generation, among whom you shine as lights in the world" (Philippians 2:15).

Romans 1:32 points out that people in the world's immoral system "not only do [evil things] but give approval to those who practice them." Some people have an affinity for people who are more wicked than they are because it makes them feel righteous by comparison. When a Christian's life or teaching rebukes another's sinfulness, they become hostile. But Jesus has called us to precisely that kind of confrontation. We cannot hide from the world what Scripture says and expect unbelievers to sense that they are indicted. We're not supposed to retreat to our churches and proclaim the gospel there but never take the message to the world. It should not be necessary for people to come into our church to hear the truth of God's Word, to be exposed to the gospel, or even to discover that we are followers of Christ. Our *lives in the world* should show it. Jesus says in Matthew 5:14 that we should be like a city that can be seen for miles because it is set on a hill. In the next verse He says that believers are like a lamp that should not be put under a basket but rather should be set on a lampstand so that it can light the entire house. Our faith should be visible to the world, not hidden away in a Sunday-school room, only to be brought out for an hour or two on Sunday.

We stand out from the world because Jesus has chosen us. In John 15:19 He tells His disciples, "I chose you out of the world." The verb in that statement is in the Greek middle voice, which gives it a reflexive meaning. Jesus is literally saying, "I chose you for myself." He has chosen us to be *different*. We are called not only to learn the Word of God and hide it in our own hearts, but also to proclaim it to the ends of the earth, to live it out before a watching world, and thereby to be a living rebuke to those in love with sin. That is always costly.

Satan does not like to *lose* anyone, and thus he moves to attack the child of God who is faithful to our calling. Peter warns Christians, "Your adversary the devil prowls around like a roaring lion, seeking someone to devour" (1 Peter 5:8). Satan pursues Christians and sets the whole world in motion against them. He hates believers as much as he hates God, because they love the righteousness the Devil hates.

I once participated in an intensive evangelization campaign on a local university campus. We shared the gospel with several thousand students. The next day the college newspaper said that unless the student group that sponsored the evangelistic effort complied with university policy by discontinuing its evangelistic work, "direct action" would be taken against the students involved. The dean had received complaints from unbelieving students who had been handed gospel tracts and challenged about their faith (or lack of it) by Christian students. The dean cited campus policy that forbade "using university facilities for religious conversion." Those were the exact words of the school's written policy regarding religion on campus. In other words, it was formally and officially against school rules for students to convert to Christianity (much less proclaim the gospel) on that campus.

No amount of discussion with campus officials could get them to see the inequity of their rules.

That is a fairly commonplace example of the way the world system resists people who want to tell the truth about sin. Anyone was free to go on that same campus and convert people to Communism, advocate for gay rights, promote abortion, peddle pornography, or do whatever wickedness or foolishness happened to be the current radical chic. Anyone who wanted to was free to organize and recruit students for any bizarre cause you can imagine, and no one would object. (If someone *did* complain, the administration would automatically defend radical free speech on the grounds of academic freedom.) But when Christian students wanted to tell people about Jesus Christ, *that* broke the rules. The world does not want to be confronted with biblical truth.

THE WORLD HATED OUR LORD

A second reason persecution is inevitable for Christians is that the world desperately hates the Lord Jesus. Christ told the eleven, "Remember the word that I said to you: 'A servant is not greater than his master.' If they persecuted me, they will also persecute you. If they kept my word, they will also keep yours" (John 15:20). Because the world hates Him, it hates those of us who name Him as Lord. Not everyone rejects Christ, and not everyone will reject us. A few will listen and believe.

Yet much of our culture's apparent acceptance of Jesus is nothing more than a facade. Most of the movies, songs, and books about Jesus written from a secular viewpoint only confuse and deceive people into thinking they understand the truth about Jesus. But no one can really know Him unless he or she knows something about sin and repentance.

There was a time in history when Christianity became politically expedient. The church had survived some two centuries of intense persecution, and then the Roman government suddenly declared it acceptable. The Roman emperor at the start of the fourth century, Constantine the Great, professed faith in Christ. Christianity became the dominant religion of the Roman Empire, and suddenly everyone who wanted Constantine's favor wanted to be "a Christian." The church was actually weakened and biblical Christianity was hurt more by the shallow popularity that resulted from those developments than the cause of truth had ever been injured by persecution. Because everyone was suddenly calling himself a Christian, no one understood how a believer's life was distinctive or what Christianity really stood for. About the same time Constantine professed Christianity, Arius, the arch-heretic, unleashed his famous attack on the deity of Christ, and within a few decades the very existence of Christianity was threatened by bishops with political interests and false teachers with deficient doctrine. The visible church became a monstrosity, an institutionalized blasphemy. But for one man, Athanasius, the whole church might have followed Arius in denying that Jesus is God. Satan welcomes that kind of confusion as much as he relishes persecuting the church.

There is a unique joy in being so identified with Jesus Christ that you suffer the rebuke, ridicule, and hatred this world directs at Him. Too many Christians today know nothing of that joy. In Philippians 3:10, Paul calls it "the fellowship of his sufferings" (KJV). First Peter 2:21 says, "For even hereunto were ye called: because Christ also suffered for us, leaving us an example, that ye should follow his steps" (KJV). But when we share His sufferings, we also share His joy over those who come to saving faith. And that makes every sacrifice worthwhile.

The World Does Not Know God

Jesus told the disciples another reason persecution must come: "All these things will they do unto you for my name's sake, because they know not him that sent me" (John 15:21). The Jewish religious leaders of Jesus' day prided themselves on what they thought was an in-depth knowledge of God. When Jesus said that they did not know God, the religious leaders were infuriated. But in rejecting Christ, they themselves proved He was right. They claimed to know God, yet they hated Christ, who was God in human flesh. Their love for God was a pretense.

What many people fail to realize is that religion itself is perhaps the greatest possible hindrance to the knowledge of the true God. The world's standard approach to religion is to postulate a god and worship him, even though that god does not exist outside man's imagination. Jesus exposed the false religion propounded by the Jewish leaders when He said, "You are of your father the devil, and your will is to do your father's desires" (John 8:44).

The problem is not that unbelieving men and women have no access to the truth about God. Romans 1:19 says, "What can be known about God is plain to them, because God has shown it to them." Both through innate knowledge and in the wonders of creation, God has given everyone basic, irrefutable knowledge that He exists. People willfully reject the truth, not because of ignorance but because they love the darkness rather than the light.

Exposing unregenerate sinners to the truth is like shining a light on an insect—the bug just wants to crawl back into the darkness.

God had given the people of Israel in Jesus' day the Old Testament and the Messiah. They heard what Christ said and saw what He did. But they killed Him. They rejected everything God could reveal to them. It was the one sin for which there could be no remedy. After seeing Him cast out a demon, a group of Pharisees said, "It is only by Beelzebul, the prince of demons, that this man casts out demons" (Matthew 12:24). They knew better, but they were determined to destroy Christ and dissuade people from following Him, no matter what (John 11:47–48). Their rejection of Him was complete and irreversible. They were knowingly repudiating the fullest possible revelation, with a deliberateness and finality that made their own repentance impossible.

Jesus then warned the Jewish leaders, "I tell you, every sin and blasphemy will be forgiven people, but the blasphemy against the Spirit will not be forgiven" (v. 31). He had done those miracles by the Holy Spirit's power. In rejecting Him and attributing His works to Satan's power, they were purposely blaspheming the Spirit. They could not be forgiven, because they had knowingly rejected full and irrefutable revelation. There was nothing more they could ever see or hear that would change their hard-hearted refusal to embrace the truth of Christ.

In John 15:25, Jesus quotes a phrase that is repeated in three Old Testament psalms (35:19; 69:4; and 109:3): "They hated me without a cause." There was no reason for the scribes and Pharisees to reject Christ. Their rejection of Him was a fulfillment of these prophetic psalms. That does not mean God desired for them to hate Jesus; but as always, He used their hatred of Jesus to further His own wise and holy ends. In this case, for example, the fulfillment of these prophecies proved that God's purposes could not be derailed by the most stubborn opposition of evil men. Their contempt for Jesus was completely without any legitimate cause. He had healed all manner of diseases; He had fed multitudes; He lived a completely sinless life. There was nothing anyone could legitimately accuse Him of, and certainly no good reason for anyone to hate Him.

Quite simply, the world hated Jesus because He exposed its sin. When His divine holiness shone on this dark world, it revealed fallen humanity's love of darkness. Instead of turning to Him in faith and love, and finding forgiveness and freedom from their sin, they turned against Him in sheer, irrational hated. In so doing, they condemned themselves.

The world is no different today. It still hates Jesus with passion. And it still hates those who truly and faithfully serve Him. If you are going to follow Him, you will have to suffer the hatred of the world. If you are unwilling, you cannot be His disciple. The price may seem high, but the rewards are much higher.

Suffering for Christ's sake is the calling of every believer (2 Timothy 3:12). He does not call any of us to a life without suffering or persecution. Suffering is a part of the cost everyone must count if he wants to be a true disciple.

Still, to be persecuted for Him is a unique privilege. It is a special joy to be identified with Christ in His suffering (Philippians 3:10). And when we truly suffer for righteousness' sake—when we are willing to be hated without a cause—that will be when we begin to understand persecution not as a thing to be resisted or avoided, but as a wonderful aspect of our fellowship with Christ.

THE LEGACY OF JESUS

All in all, Jesus has left His disciples quite a legacy. He gave us the supreme example of humble love when He washed the disciples' feet.

And He left us a complete array of promises: the hope of heaven; the permanent, indwelling presence of the Holy Spirit; truth, peace, fruitfulness, joy, spiritual power; and even the guarantee that He stands with us when we are persecuted.

All of those things belong to every true disciple of Christ. Consider again our Lord's gracious words: "I will not leave you as orphans; I will come to you. Yet a little while and the world will see me no more, but you will see me. Because I live, you also will live. In that day you will know that I am in my Father, and you in me, and I in you" (John 14:18–20).